Charles Theodore Russell, Erastus Everett

Celebration of the One Hundredth Anniversary

Of the Incorporation of the Town of Princeton, Mass., October 20th, 1859

Charles Theodore Russell, Erastus Everett

Celebration of the One Hundredth Anniversary
Of the Incorporation of the Town of Princeton, Mass., October 20th, 1859

ISBN/EAN: 9783337168032

Printed in Europe, USA, Canada, Australia, Japan

Cover: Foto ©Andreas Hilbeck / pixelio.de

More available books at **www.hansebooks.com**

CELEBRATION

OF THE

ONE HUNDREDTH ANNIVERSARY

OF THE

INCORPORATION

OF THE

TOWN OF PRINCETON, MASS.

OCTOBER 20th, 1859.

INCLUDING THE ADDRESS

OF

HON. CHARLES THEODORE RUSSELL,

THE POEM OF

PROF. ERASTUS EVERETT,

AND

OTHER EXERCISES OF THE OCCASION.

~~~~~~~~~~~~~~~~~~~~~~~~~~

"He who regards not the memory and character of his ancestors, deserves to be forgotten by posterity."

~~~~~~~~~~~~~~~~~~~~~~~~~~

WORCESTER:
TRANSCRIPT OFFICE, WM. R. HOOPER, PRINTER.
1860.

ACTION OF THE TOWN.

Pursuant to a warrant issued by the Selectmen of the Town, upon the petition of fifteen legal voters thereof, a town meeting was held at Boylston Hall, on the 22d day of September, 1859, at which meeting it was voted to celebrate the one hundreth anniversary of the incorporation of the town, on the 20th day of October next, with services and observances suitable to such an occasion. And the following persons were chosen a committee to make all necessary arrangements for the same, viz.:

At Large.—George F. Folger, Addison Smith, John Brooks, Jr., Wilkes Roper, Charles A. Whittaker, George E. Pratt, Edward E. Hartwell, John C. Davis, Ivory Wilder, Joseph M. Stewart.

By Districts.—No. 1, Harlow Skinner; 2, Abram Everett; 3, William H. Brown; 4, Otis Wood; 5, Paul Garfield; 6, George Mason; 7, Samuel Roper; 8, Artemas J. Brooks; 9, William B. Goodnow; 10, Joshua T. Everett.

At a subsequent meeting of the town, held at Boylston Hall, on the 8th day of November, "Voted, to publish in book form the exercises of the late Centennial Celebration;" and chose the following a committee to carry the same into effect:

Committee.—Joshua T. Everett, Charles Russell, William B. Goodnow, Edward E. Hartwell, Albert C. Howe.

An organization of the Committee of Arrangements was effected by the choice of William B. Goodnow, Chairman, and Edward E. Hartwell, Secretary. Sub-committees wero appointed, to whom special duties were assigned; and the following persons were unanimously chosen as the officers of the day:

PRESIDENT OF THE DAY.

Hon. CHARLES RUSSELL.

VICE PRESIDENTS.

Hon. JOHN BROOKS,
ISRAEL EVERETT,
CALEB S. MIRICK,
Dea. HENRY BOYLES,
EBENEZER SMITH,
JOHN G. HOBBS,
MOSES GARFIELD,

Dr. ALPHONSO BROOKS,
JOSEPH MASON,
SOLON S. HASTINGS, Esq.,
Dr. WARD N. BOYLSTON,
RUFUS DAVIS,
DANIEL DAVIS,
FREDERICK PARKER.

TOAST MASTER.
JOSHUA T. EVERETT.

CHIEF MARSHAL.
WILLIAM B. GOODNOW.

ASSISTANTS.

HARLOW SKINNER,
WILLIAM H. BROWN,
GEORGE E. PRATT,
JONAS B. BROWN,
JOHN BROOKS, Jr.,

EDWARD E. HARTWELL,
GEORGE F. FOLGER,
OTIS WOOD,
CHARLES T. MIRICK,
ADDISON SMITH,

ARTEMAS J. BROOKS.

CHAPLAINS.
Rev. HUMPHREY MOORE, D. D., Rev. DAVID O. ALLEN, D. D.

THE CELEBRATION.

Princeton welcomed home her native and adopted sons, October 20th, 1859, to a festival long to be remembered, in commemoration of her one hundredth birthday. As a stand-point from which to look backward and forward, the occasion is deeply suggestive, and the exercises of the day were, in a very satisfactory degree, interesting and impressive.

The weather was unusually cold for the season, yet warm hearts were ready to greet, and were as warmly greeted in return. A family gathering—scattered East and West, North and South—the good old grandmother could hardly expect to see *all* "who have gone out from her, but who are yet *of* her," present; but a very large number, from those whose whitened locks proclaimed them the friends of her earlier years, to those who could hardly lisp her name, were there, to exchange kindly salutations, to revive old, yet none the less pleasing, associations, and unite in ascriptions of praise to the Father of Mercies, for giving so " goodly a heritage."

OUT-DOOR DEMONSTRATIONS.

The festivities of the day commenced with the firing of cannon, the parade of citizens, under the escort of the Wachusett Cornet Band, and other public manifestations of rejoicing. The streets and many of the buildings on the hill were handsomely decorated, under the superin-

tendence of Col. Beals, of Boston. The Wachusett Hotel
saluted visitors as they came up the hill, with the motto,
over its portico, " We welcome you home," and the house itself was profusely ornamented. Across the Common were
suspended the flags of all nations, and the Union Congrega-
tional Church was gaily decorated with the Colonel's most
impressive combination of colors, while in the recess in
front hung a full length portrait of "The Father of his
Country." Over the pulpit was placed the motto, which
told the whole story of the celebration:

" Princeton Incorporated Oct. 20th, 1759."
and other appropriate memorial emblems and mottoes
were displayed throughout the town.

PROCESSION.

At 10 o'clock A. M., a procession was formed on the
Common, under the direction of the Chief Marshal, William
B. Goodnow, and his aids, in the following order:

Aid.   Chief Marshal.   Aid.
Escort.
Thirty of the Sons of Princeton.
Music — Wachusett Cornet Band.
President of the day, Orator and Poet.
Chaplains, Vice Presidents and Invited Guests.
Rutland Brass Band.
Rutland delegation, under the direction of Col.
Calvin G. Howe as Marshal.
Citizens of Princeton and other towns.

The boisterous weather made it necessary to repair to
the church, (Rev. Wm. T. Briggs',) whither the procession
was conducted, and where the chief exercises were held.

EXERCISES AT THE CHURCH.

When the large audience—filling both aisles and galleries to overflowing—had assembled, William B. Goodnow, Chief Marshal, called the meeting to order, and introduced the President of the day, Hon. Charles Russell, who, in coming forward, spoke briefly and in a congratulatory manner of the pleasant circumstances which had called them together; regretting that they had not now the large and spacious church built by their fathers more than sixty years ago, but which had now passed away. He craved the indulgence of the audience while they made the best use of the accommodations they had. He then called attention to the exercises of the day, which were as follows:

I.—Music by the Band.

II.—A Voluntary by the Choir.

III.—Reading of select portions of the Scriptures by Rev. Wm. T. Briggs.

IV.—Prayer by Rev. Humphrey Moore, D. D., of Milford, N. II.

V.—An original Hymn, composed for the occasion by Joseph W. Nye, of East Princeton, was sung by the Choir.

HYMN.

Not as they met—those pioneers,
  One hundred years ago to-day,
Meet we, as close those many years,
  Our tribute of respect to pay ;
They met, a brave but feeble band,
Where now a number great we stand.

Here, where the savage loved to roam,
  Amid the dim old solitudes,
Hath education found a home ;
  And echo now these "grand old woods,"
With music such as science brings,
Where'er she spreads her golden wings !

No longer dormant lay the fields,
  Stirred by the farmer's clearing plough,
The pasture wild a harvest yields,
  Rewarding well his sweaty brow ;
And yearly doth the fruitful soil,
Repay him for his days of toil !

And still with ever watchful eye,
　　Our loved high priest, "Wachusett," stands,
While fruitful vales around him lie,
　　Baptised in plenty at his hands;
He waves his censor, and the gale,
The fragrance beareth through the vale!

God of Creation! bless us here,
　　As on this festal day we come;
Be Thou to guide us ever near,
　　And take us to Thy heavenly home
When all our meetings here are o'er,
To worship Thee forevermore.

And when another hundred years,
　　Have rolled upon their course sublime,
When all our earthly joys and fears
　　Have disappeared with fading time;
Here may our children's children meet,
And joyfully this scene repeat!

After this, the following Oration was delivered by Hon.
Charles T. Russell, of Boston.

ORATION

BY HON. CHARLES T. RUSSELL.

———

One hundred years ago, to-day, the few and scattered dwellers about the base of Wachusett, received from the Colonial Legislature, and the Royal Governor, the act which gave them a place and a name among the municipal corporations of Massachusetts. Here and now, upon the soil they settled and subdued, not far from the humble tavern where they held their first town meeting, we, their children, meet on the old and loved homestead, in joyful commemoration of the centennial birthday of our town.

Gathering on this autumnal morning, at home and from abroad, not strangers nor the public, but townsmen, friends, fathers, mothers, brothers, sisters—a family circle, around the family fireside—at a family festival, our thoughts irresistibly turn to family matters. Here, on a Thanksgiving day, seated, as it were, on the settle, by the dear old chimney corner, while the dinner is cooking, cold and strange would it be, indeed, did we not talk of family history, with minuteness, even, of remembrance and incident.

We come, at a mother's kindly call, with a child's filial heart, to meet *her*, dearer by every wrinkle time sets upon her brow, in *her own home*. It is but the impulse of her

2

early instructions, the first warm greetings over, that we reverently bow before our Maker, at her knee, and with the earnestness of childhood, adopt its consecrated words, and

> Thank the goodness and the grace,
> That on our birth have smiled,
> And in these Christian days,
> Made each a free and happy child.

Rising from this grateful duty to other service, insensate should we be, did not our hearts, in this interview of filial and parental love, break forth in blessings many, and too strong, perhaps, for stranger ears, upon her who so kindly cared for our youth, and so sweetly smiles on our manhood.

In our most public proceedings, to-day, we are but townsmen, in town meeting assembled. No article in our warrant authorizes any business but of immediate domestic concernment, and I should be instantly called to order by universal shout, were I to attempt to speak of aught but our own early history, being allowed, of course, to refer to those larger and more general events, which have entered into, modified and shaped it.

Standing where our fathers stood a hundred years ago, removed from them by a century, the most stirring, active and marvellous, in its progress, history and developments, of any since the Christian era, we find our town sharing always in the general advance quite up to the standard of an agricultural and conservative community, still in all that is peculiar, as little changed as any in the Commonwealth. Yet how grand and striking the contrasts made by mere circumstances, the changes of time, and the progress of knowledge and events, between the days of them, the fathers, and us, the children.

In the middle of the eighteenth century, the hostile warwhoop had ceased to be heard in the "wilderness country, beyond the Nashua," and around the Wachusett. Sholan no longer kept his royal seat, in sight from this hill, between the Washacums. Lancaster had risen from the ashes in which the Narragansett war had laid it. Worcester sent out no bodies of soldiery on the report that large numbers of Indians "hovered between it and Wachusett Mountain." And yet of the first settler in Princeton, the grandfather had been killed, and the father attacked by these same savages; and the daughter, born as late as 1739, recollected to have gathered blueberries on this very hill with a file of soldiers for protection. Men, younger than many I now address, remembered the Indian fight in Sterling, and the burning of the church and last attacks at Lancaster—remembrances, events just then occurring, might well quicken and impress.

But if the savages, as enemies, had retired, the forest was present. Looking from this eminence, on the 20th of October, 1759, the eye rested upon a wilderness, clothed in all the gorgeous beauty of a New England Autumn, —but unbroken in its whole extent save where some distant pond glittered in the sunlight, or the curling smoke revealed the settler's dwelling, or the smouldering fires of the pioneer's clearing. Hubbardston, Sterling and Boylston were not. Westminster was but a twin born sister. No roads threaded these primeval woods. And dweller found dweller, in traffic, mutual aid or social intercourse, by the bridle path and marked tree, escorted by an occasional wolf or growling bear. No mail—no weekly postman, even, brought news from the inner world to these outside settlers. What they learned of the distant homes they had left *away down to Shrewsbury, Lancaster and Weston and Watertown,* they gathered by chance visits, or the letter some friendly hand casually brought. The Boston Weekly Newspaper, which found its way occasionally to some of them, told them from time to time, of the stirring events transpiring around them, and in the distant country to which they owed allegiance.

Our fathers were the subjects of Great Britain. The act which made them a town, and the warrant which called them together to organize it, were alike in the name of the second George. Lightly, as in their forest homes, their allegiance ordinarily sat upon them,—there was a peculiar significance to it just now. They were in the midst of sharing actively the first great contest for civil liberty on the continent. Their sovereign was its leader, and king and colonist, cemented by a common interest, alike unconscious of the fact, were laying broad and deep the foundation of future freedom.

Hardly more than a century since, France, by military posts and possessions, had drawn a narrowing circle around the English Colonies, and, in a magnificent sweep, claimed jurisdiction from the Gulf of St. Lawrence to that of Mexico. On the Saguenay and Ottawa, amid the solitary grandeur of Niagara, at Champlain, and along the whole line of inland waters from Ontario to Michigan, the rude cross marked her faith, and the *fleur de lis* asserted her power. Her soldiery struggled with Washington for the beautiful basin of the Ohio. " In the whole valley of the Mississippi, to its head springs in the Alleghanies, no standard floated but hers." The institutions of the middle ages and rising liberty confronted each other in the primeval forest and untrampled prairie. What race should people these vast solitudes, what language make them vocal,—feudalism or freedom, Catholicism or Protestantism, which should take root in this virgin soil,—these were the grand issues of that contest Washington opened at Great Meadows, and Wolfe closed at Quebec.

Long before Marquette, La Salle and Hennepin had explored the Mississippi, from the falls of St. Anthony to its mouth, and reared along its solitary banks the arms of France. French forts were established at Champlain, Ontario, Niagara, Erie, and finally on the sources of the Ohio at Pittsburg, while the unbroken forests swarmed with their Indian allies, from the shores of the lakes to the frowning ramparts of Quebec. Massachusetts not long back had mourned French and savage inroads, of which she dreaded the renewal, at points within our view to-day.

They had roused the peaceful Quaker spirit of Pennsylvania, and the more ardent vigor of Virginia and New York. The races approached, the lines were drawn, the posts taken, the crisis impended, and the rattle of Washington's musketry in the western wilderness " broke the repose of the world," and, as has been well said, " began the battle, which was to banish from the soil and neighborhood of our republic the institutions of the middle age, and to inflict on them fatal wounds throughout the continent of Europe."

In 1750, the French and English Commissioners at Paris had failed to settle the boundaries of their North American territory by negotiation. In 1754, Washington surrendered at Fort Necessity. The year following, Massachusetts troops secured Nova Scotia, and became associated with, if they did not incur, the infamy of removing the peaceful Acadians. Braddock, self-willed and impracticable, met his disastrous defeat in the forests of Fort Du Quesne. In 1756, war was finally declared between England and France, and the chivalric Montcalm assumed the French command in America. Pushing through the forest and along Lake Ontario, while Loudoun and Abercrombie lingered at Albany, he captured the fort at Oswego, reared upon its ruins the cross, and by its side a pillar, bearing the arms of France, and the inscription, " Bring lilies with full hands."

Flushed with success, the next year he descended the shores of Lake George upon Fort William Henry, with eight thousand French and Indians, where the gallant Monro maintained a death struggle, till half his guns were burst and his ammunition all expended. In August of that year, Massachusetts issued an order, " for all and every one of his Majesty's well affected subjects, able to bear arms, to repair to Fort Edward, on the Hudson, to serve with Gen. Webb, for the relief of Fort William Henry, which still stands out fighting against a large and numerous body of the enemy." Already the regiments of the counties of

Hampshire and Worcester had gone forward to the relief of Monro, and, with their associates in arms, but for the inefficiency of Webb, might have saved us the sad disaster of that broken-hearted officer's surrender.

Just then, in the language of another, " The English had been driven from every cabin in the basin of the Ohio. Montcalm had destroyed every vestige of their power within that of the St. Lawrence." " Of the North American Continent, the French claimed, and seemed to possess, twenty parts in twenty-five, leaving four only to Spain and but one to Britain." England herself, straining every nerve to exhaustion, to aid the great protestant power, then developing itself under Frederic,—borne down by an incompetent ministry, which distrusted the colonies, and was repudiated by the people, seemed incapable of turning the tide of American affairs. Massachusetts, through all her borders, trembled for her security, and the dwellers in her more unsettled interior, recalled, with fearful forebodings, savage inroads within their personal recollection, and from causes again active.

At this moment of disaster and gloom, England's great commoner assumed the guidance of her counsels, and accomplished some of the brightest glories of her history. Entering permanently upon his administration in 1757, challenging the support of the colonies by a generous confidence, throwing to the winds the fears, and boldly reversing the maxims of his predecessors, he matured and executed those plans, which crowned the first great American conflict with the entire subjugation of French America.

Animated by his justice, and their confidence in him, the Colonies rallied at once to his support. Massachusetts sent seven thousand troops to the army of that year, and had enrolled nearly one-third of all her effective men. In July, Amherst, seconded by Wolfe, captured Louisburg, and in the same month the gallant Howe fell at Lake George, and Abercrombie retreated, disastrously repulsed by Montcalm from Ticonderoga. In November, Forbes, prompted and sustained by the energetic spirit of Washington, took Fort Duquesne, and as his country's flag rose over it, gave it the name of that country's protector. The persevering Bradstreet rescued Abercrombie's division from entire disaster by the subjugation of Fort Frontenac, on Lake Ontario.

In 1759, in the steady march of events, Niagara, Ticonderoga and Crown Point were taken by the English, and the French driven back upon the St. Lawrence. Montcalm repaired to Quebec, where his sagacious mind saw the decisive blow must be met, and awaited it in fearless but foreboding self-possession. On the 13th of September it fell, and Wolfe, noblest and bravest of British officers, over unprecedented obstacles, achieved, with his life, on the plains of Abraham, the first decisive victory of American liberty on the battle field. Our fathers, in their humble homes in the forest, received, with their act of incorporation, the grateful tidings just then sending a thrill of exultant joy throughout the Colonies, and which emancipated them from the further power or fear of French or Indian.

Such were the times and scenes amid which our fathers lived. Such the stirring circumstances and grand events transpiring around them,—not distant and remote and to them indifferent,—but upon their very frontier, and threatening home and fireside. They shared the duties and dangers of the field, and in almost every household, nearly or more remotely mourned its losses. One has only to run over the muster rolls of Chandler, Ruggles and others to see how largely all this region of Worcester County participated in the French wars, and how largely they suffered from them. It is a somewhat curious and interesting fact that the first settler of Princeton made himself bankrupt by a purchase of cattle for the supply of the British army in Canada.

I have detained you longer, perhaps, than I ought, especially after my promises in the beginning, with these larger and more general events. I have done so because occurring just at the period of their incorporation, they illustrated the times in which our fathers lived, enter into their domestic history, affected their homes and firesides, and were the familiar subjects which filled up the talks of their winter evenings.

But it is quite time I should turn to history purely our own. In doing so, I desire to say that the short time allowed me for preparation has not permitted me to make all the investigations I could desire—or even to complete all upon which I have entered. I have, however, found several valuable papers and maps, that I supposed were not in existence, and which throw much light upon our early history, and correct some errors in regard to it.

The territory composing our town, although not settled or incorporated till a comparatively late period, was yet early known and somewhat explored. Wachusett, as the highest land in the State, became not only an object of interest but a landmark for all the surrounding country. Centuries before a white man set foot upon it, such was it to its savage possessors and frequenters. Could its venerable summit speak to us of all it has witnessed, while for ages it looked

"Upon the green and rolling forest tops,
And down into the secrets of the glens,"

before the eye of civilized being rested upon it, what a history might it unfold! How much of Indian life and action, love and hate, fidelity and treachery, worship, cruelty, decay and extinction! What tribes have held its sovereignty, what wild tenants thronged its precincts, what scenes of peace or war it has witnessed, how long it stood in solitary grandeur before human foot pressed its rocky soil,—what captives have been tortured or released at its base,—what assaults and murders planned upon its sides, what settlements marked and devoted from its top, who gave it the name, you, with such good taste, refuse to change, and witnessed its baptism, far back

> " When the gray chief and gifted seer,
> Worshipped the God of thunders here."

We may interrogate it, but we shall interrogate it in vain. Everything that has transpired on and around it, from the lighting of the first Indian fire in its forests, to the last tale of love whispered in the pale-faced maiden's ear, at sunset, on its summit, is sacredly locked in its faithful bosom, as arrayed in the splendor of its autumnal robes, it looks down, in serene and silent majesty upon our services to-day.

Were those venerable sides now to break their long silence, and essay to speak, dead and living would join in equal and earnest protest, from the first mountain Hiawatha, who there laid the red deer at his Minnehaha's feet, to the last Summer visitor who there breathed words of love to his Genevieve, till she too

> " Said and blushed to say it,
> I will follow you, my husband."

And

> " Hand in hand, they went together,
> Through the woodland and the meadow."

The first reference to Wachusett, unless we adopt the suggestion that it is the hill laid down by John Smith in his map in 1616, is by Gov. Winthrop, in 1632. On the 27th of January, of that year, "the Governor and some company with him," says his journal, "went up Charles River about eight miles above Watertown," where "they went up a very high rock, from whence they might see all over Neipnett, and a very high hill due west about forty miles off." Probably this is the first specific mention of any portion of the territory of Worcester County, as its wilderness was never traversed by civilized man, until the expedition toward Connecticut, in 1635.

In 1643, Governor Winthrop again says, " At this court, Nashacowam and Wassamagoin, two sachems near the great hill to the west, called (Warehasset,) Wachusett, came into the court, and, according to their former tender to the Governor, desired to be received under our protection and government, upon the same terms that Pomhom and Saconoco were ; so we, causing them to understand the articles, and all the ten commandments of God, and they, freely assenting to all, they were solemnly received, and then presented the court with twenty-six fathom more of wampum, and the court gave each of them a coat of two yards of cloth and their dinner; and to them and their men, every one of them a cup of sack at their departure ; so they took leave and went away very joyful."

At this time the Nipmucks owned and occupied most of the region now making the south part of Worcester County. How far their domain extended, and what were the precise relations between them and the Nashaways, who held the territory along the Nashua and about the Wachusett, is uncertain. The sachem of the latter was Sholan, or Shawman, who had his royal residence, if that term may be applied to a wigwam and corn patch, on the neck of land between the Washacums, in our sight to-day. To his barbaric dominion our territory was subject. During this year, upon his invitation, King and others of Watertown, purchased of him a tract ten miles by eight on the Nashua, and began the settlement of Lancaster. This preceded by many years any other town in Worcester County, and was for a half century the nearest settlement to Wachusett.

In February, 1676, the Indians of this region, among whom were those who had received the pious instruction of Eliot and Gookin, instigated by Philip, joined in the Narragansett war. Assembling in large numbers, they made the disastrous attack upon Lancaster, so familiar to us from the simple and touching narrative of Mrs. Rowlandson. "After many weary steps," says this trusting Christian woman, returning from sufferings and wanderings in the wilderness, "we came to Wachusett." It would seem that she remained here with a body of Indians during the attack upon Sudbury, and she describes the pow-wow preliminary to that assault. After this, she says, three or four miles distant from the mountain, "they built a great wigwam, big enough to hold an hundred Indians, which they did in preparation to a great day of dancing." "They began now to come from all quarters against the merry dancing day." This is the first public celebration within the limits or vicinage of our town of which we have any history. For a curious account of the services, I must refer you to the lady's narrative.

Meantime, Mr. Hoar had come to secure her ransom, and we have a statement of some diplomatic social intercourse, which rather unfavorably reflects upon our Indian predecessors. "In the morning," says Mrs. Rowlandson, "Mr. Hoar invited the Sagamores to dinner; but when we went to get it ready, we found they had stolen the greater part of the provisions Mr. Hoar had brought, and we may see the wonderful power of God, in that one passage, in that when there was such a number of them together, and so greedy of a little good food, and no English there, but Mr. Hoar and myself, that it was a wonder they did not knock us on the head, and take what we had."

Here the Indians called their General Court which finally consented to release Mrs. Rowlandson.

Shortly after, the General Court of the Province, sent Seth Perry as a special messenger to them, and by him a letter addressed to "The Sagamore about Wachusetts, Phillip, John, Sam, Washaken, old Queen and Pomhom." It would seem from this that Mr. Hoar brought letters from them, suing for peace, for it speaks of receiving their letters, and adds, "In your letter to us you say you desire not to be hindered by our men in your planting, promising not to do damage to our towns. If you will send us home all the English prisoners, it will be a great testimony of a true heart in you to peace."

The same year, in a letter to the Council at Hartford, the General Court say, that it was their intention to have left a sufficient garrison at Sudbury and Marlboro', and "have drawn their forces to visit, had it been feasible, the *headquarters* of the enemy at Wachusetts ;" but divine Providence ordered it that their forces "by weakness and wants could not attayne that end." They add, we "hope by the first of June to be out with five hundred horse and foot and Indians, on the visiting of the ennemye's headquarters at Wachusetts, taking it in the march to Hadley."

At this time, beyond doubt, our town was the headquarters of the hostile Indians.

In 1681, Mr. Stoughton and Joseph Dudley were appointed by the Court to negotiate with the Nipmucks for their territory. In February of the next year they report that they have purchased of black James, one tract for thirty pounds and a coat, and for fifty pounds, another tract fifty miles long and twenty wide. "The northern part towards Wachusett " they say "is still unpurchased, and persons yet scarcely to be found meet to be treated with thereabouts."

Four years later, Henry Willard, Joseph Rowlandson, Joseph Foster, Benjamin Willard and Cyprian Stevens made the purchase of Puagastion, Pompamamey, Wananapan, Sassawannow and Qualipunit of " a certain tract of lands, Medows, Swamps, Timbers, Etervils, containing twelve miles square," and known as Naquag. For this they paid twenty-three pounds—which is much higher than the Province paid for the Nipmuck territory, four years before. Although the price is but eighty cents a square mile, it seems to have been quite up to the market, as fixed by the sale of "adjoining lots." How the grantees discovered the title of these Indian grantors, which escaped the vigilance of the Provincial Commissioners, or what the title was does not appear. The savages backed their title with very ample covenants of seizin, and set their marks to warranties of the strongest form.

This purchase included what is now Rutland, Hubbardston, Barre, Oakham, a part of Paxton, and the larger half of Princeton. Its northerly line ran nearly a mile north of where we are now assembled, across the whole of the town, to " Greate Wachusett," excluding, however, that mountain. The Indian deed was probably worthless till confirmed by the General Court, and it seems to have been so regarded. We hear nothing of it from its date till 1713. During the intervening period, the Indians possessed or frequented the territory. As late as 1704, an attack was made upon Lancaster, and the Church burnt, and in 1707 the Indian fight, as it is called, occurred in Sterling. Occasional ruptures and murders continued up to 1710.

As late as 1725, Capt. Brintnall was ordered to surround and protect with his company, the meadows in Rutland, while the farmers gathered their hay.

In 1714, the General Court, upon the application of the sons and grandsons of Maj. Simon Willard, and others, confirmed to them the land described in the Indian deed, provided there should be sixty families settled thereon in seven years, and " sufficient lands reserved for the use of a gospel minister and school." On the 14th of April of that year, the proprietors held their first meeting, and the Indian deed was put upon record. In 1716, six miles square, constituting the present town of Rutland, was set off for the settlers required by the condition of the confirmation, and measures taken to secure them. The other portions of the territory were soon after divided into wings or quarters. Of these the east wing constitutes the southerly and larger part of Princeton.

There are three plans of this Naquag or Rutland purchase, on file in the archives of the Commonwealth, at the State House. The last is a very accurate one, presented by Rev. Thomas Prince and others, a committee of the propri-

etors, on the occasion of asking the grant of a land tax in
1749. Upon this the several wings or quarters are all laid
down. The east wing is a parallelogram nearly, all its lines
being perfectly straight, the east and west each eleven hundred and fifty rods, the south sixteen hundred and ninety
rods, and the north sixteen hundred rods. Its area varies
somewhat on these and the later plans, a fact not surprising
in those days of liberal allowance " for sags of the chain." It
contained about eleven thousand and seven huudred acres,
and the north line separating it from the Province lands, then
unsurveyed and extending far beyond, ran straight from
the south-east corner of what was subsequently known as
the letter M lot, to the extreme south-west edge of Wachusett. The Meeting-House Hill was then called Turkey
Hill, and this line ran along the depression between the two
Wachusetts, where the road now passes.

This tract remained in common, neither surveyed nor
explored, until 1718, when it was divided by the proprietors
into forty-eight farms, of two hundred and thirty-seven
acres each. At this time there were thirty-three proprietors, and at a meeting in Boston, November 5, of that year,
one of these farms was assigned to each by lot. The three
meadow lots, Pout Water, Wachusett, and Dead Meadow,
were reserved for common use. Twelve lots, marked by
letters from A to M, were also reserved, eleven for the
proprietors, the other "for the first ordained minister of
Rutland." The full list of the proprietors, with the lot of
each, is recorded in their records.

The lettered lots were owned in common until September
24th, 1734, when, at a meeting of the proprietors at the
Royal Exchange Tavern, Boston, these lots, together with
the "gores and gussets," as the records have it, were divided.
At the same meeting, it was voted that sixty-three acres
" in lot No. A, (this included the Meeting-House Hill,) not
having been set off to any of the proprietors, by reason
of the brokenness of it, be granted to Rev. Mr. Thomas
Prince, in consideration of the great care and labor he has

taken in calculating and computing the divisions above mentioned, and other good services performed to the proprietors."

In November, 1736, the Wachusett, Pout Water and Dead Meadow lots were divided, in the division, one acre of meadow being "valued as three acres of upland." Thus, the whole territory became subdivided and passed to individuals. Of these the Rev. Mr. Prince, as the proprietor of five shares, was the largest owner, although he does not appear to have been a proprietor at the division in 1718. Probably still further purchases were made by him before 1759.

The northerly and remaining portion of the town, comprising at its incorporation, seven thousand two hundred and eighty-three acres, is composed of several distinct grants, the history of which time does not permit me to give in detail. The largest and most important was made to the towns of Weston and Watertown. Its circumstances and date have been inaccurately stated heretofore, as I find by the original documents, to which I have recently had access.

In 1651, Watertown, then embracing Weston, was involved in a controversy with Sudbury, as to boundaries, which the General Court settled in favor of Sudbury. At the same time it passed an order that "Water Toune shall have two thousand ackers of land laid out nere Assabeth River, in respect of such land as was wanting to them, which was granted them formerly by this Court to be the bounds of their toune."

For some reason, this grant never took effect, or was never located. In 1728, Watertown and Weston, which had then been incorporated, petitioned to have it revived; and in June of that year, the General Court granted to those towns two thousand acres, to be located in any unappropriated lands of the Province. In November it was selected, surveyed, and a plan returned to the General Court. In this it is described as "in the unappropriated land, joining to the

Great Watchusett Hill, bounded south.westerly by Rutland line of their township, every other way by Province land." This tract ran on Rutland line eight hundred and forty rods, or a little more than two and a half miles. Its lines are all strait except the west, which is very daintily deflected to exclude the mountain, and at the same, include all the valuable land at its base. Wachusett was no favorite with the land seekers, who alike closed their inhospitable lines against it, thrusting it into cold exclusion, till some enterprising surveyor should bring it in, by a gigantic sag of the chain, or some masterly deduction.

This tract, commencing at a point on the line of Rutland East Wing, a little south-easterly of the Whitney Hill, extended to East Princeton, including a part of that village, and thence over, or to the north of Pine Hill, to the base of Wachusett, and thence along this to the Rutland line. It was known as the Watertown Farm, and is usually so called in public documents of the time. It was sold by the towns to proprietors, and by them divided into farms of equal value.

Another large grant of fifteen hundred acres was made to Thomas Plaisted. This tract is usually called the Potash Farm, in the public records. When granted, or for what purpose, I have been unable to ascertain as yet. It seems that Plaisted did not fulfill the conditions of the grant, for in 1760, the General Court directed William Richardson to demand of Timothy Mosman possession of the "fifteen hundred acres granted Plaisted on certain conditions which were not fulfilled by him." In 1761, they sent a committee to prevent and prosecute the encroachments of Lancaster upon this farm—that town, then including Sterling, claiming some part of it to be within her bounds. In 1762, an attempt was made to sell this, a farm of eighty acres west of it, and the Wachusett, at auction, putting them up at a limited minimum price. The same year, Ezra Taylor, as a committee, came up and run the lines of the Potash Farm, and reported that he found the most valuable part of the timber cut, and adds, " I can't find out any person who has done it, except one Timothy Mosman, who was then in possession."

In 1764, the General Court, on the last day of its session, granted the farm to Gen. Timothy Ruggles, the speaker, " in testimony of their grateful sense of the important services he rendered his country during the late war."

Besides these larger, there were various grants to individuals. In 1729, three hundred acres to Rev. Joseph Willard, of Rutland, and two hundred to Benjamin Muzzy. In 1732, four hundred to Rev. Benjamin Allen, and two hundred, in 1733, to Joseph Stevens, and one hundred and twenty to Joshua Wilder, Jr., in 1743. There were also the Blagrow and the Mayhew farms, and there was included in the town at the incorporation, a considerable area of Province land, of which the mountain was part.

As early as 1734, some votes were passed by the Rutland proprietors, in reference to " bringing forward settlements in the East Wing," but none were made. The first settlement in Princeton was not upon this territory, nor upon the Watertown farm, but by an enterprising pioneer upon a grant he obtained from the Province. This settlement, I think, from evidence in my possession, must have been made three or four years later than has been supposed. Joshua Wilder, Jr., has been generally understood to have been the first settler. He was the grandson of Capt. Nathaniel Wilder, of Lancaster, a man of some celebrity in his time, and grandson of the elder Nathaniel, who was killed in one of the Indian attacks upon that town. He commenced, and for many years occupied, the farm more recently owned by the late Peabody Houghton, and has been generally stated to have settled there as early as 1739. But I find on the files at the State House, a petition from him to the General Court at the May session in 1742, wherein he sets forth, " That the distance between Lancaster and a new town called Nichewaug is about twenty-five miles. That about ten miles west of Lancaster Meeting-House there is a track of Province land, which contains about one hundred and twenty acres, lying between land formerly granted to Mr. Plaisted and Allen, and a farm called Blagrows farm, which lys out of the bounds of any Town."

"That your petitioner, though a poor man, yet he humbly apprehends he hath the character of an Honest and Laborious man, and is minded to settle himself and family thereon."

"That, therefore, he is very desirous of obtaining a grant of said land on such conditions as may be consistent with your Excellency's and Honorable wisdom, on as easy terms as may be, and should he obtain it, he apprehends it would be of great service to people travelling from Lancaster to the new towns now settling westward, to have a house to depart to in their travelling."

Upon this petition, the General Court, April 7th, 1743, ordered that the land be granted, provided the petitioner "does within one year have a good and convenient house built thereon for the accommodation of Travellers, and have ten acres thereof cleared and brought to English grass or plowing within four years, and that he dwell thereon with his family, or have one other good family dwell thereon."

This grant must have been the farm on which Wilder settled. If so, he came here in 1743, and not 1739. I presume this was the first settlement in town, and such would be the natural inference from the statements of Wilder's petition, and the reasons and conditions upon which the grant was made. Nishewaug, Petersham, was being settled at this time, and from its frontier and exposed situation, was an object of interest to the government, and it is stated by the historian of Worcester County, that "there were no settled towns nearer than Lancaster on the east, and Rutland to the south-east, and Brookfield to the south, except a few new settlers in Hardwick." The first settlement of our town had thus something of public interest about it, and was in aid of the pioneer emigrants to the then nearest West.

Mr. Wilder occupied his farm till after the incorporation, when, having lost his property by a speculation in cattle for the supply of the army in Canada, he sold out and removed to Cold Spring, now Belchertown, where he died in 1762.

The next settler, and the first in the Rutland part, was Abijah Moore, who began the farm, now occupied by Major Joseph A. Read, in 1750. Here Mr. Moore, who subsequently became a leading man in town and church, shortly after opened a tavern, the first in the place, unless Mr. Wilder's wilderness station had that character. Probably both had reference to the same wants of settlers beyond.

The third inhabitant was Mr. Cheever, who occupied the Cobb Farm, in the southerly part of the East Wing. The next settlement was in the extreme north-west, between Wachusett and the pond, on the farm more recently occupied by Luther Goodnow. This was made by Robert Keyes, who came there from Shrewsbury. I think it quite probable Mr. Keyes was connected with the first settler by marriage, as Mr. Wilder's wife was the daughter of Major John Keyes of Shrewsbury.

These early settlements were in opposite extremes of the town. Each was distant from its nearest neighbor some two miles, and two double that. Two were in Rutland, and two upon Province land, not in any town or district.

Mr. Keyes was somewhat noted as a hunter, and this character may have guided his choice of a locality in the woods, under the Wachusett. His settlement became more notorious than the others, by the fact that, shortly after, he lost a daughter, who strayed into the woods, following her older sisters who had gone to the neighboring pond. The country, for many miles round, was rallied to search the forest for her, and the pond was dragged; but no traces or tidings of her were ever had. It was generally believed then and since that she was carried off by Indians.

I have recently found upon the files of the General Court, a petition from Mr. Keyes, presented in 1765, in which he says, that "in ye year of 1755 he lost one of his children, and was supposed to be taken by the Indians and carried to Canada. When it was first lost, it was apprehended to be in the woods, wandering about, and your petitioner was at great cost and trouble in searching the woods for it, but to no good purpose; after this, he hears that it was at Canada, and that he could get further information thereof at Porch Mouth, in New Hampshire; on hearing that he went there, and also sent to Canada afterwards. He advertised said child in the New York papers; upon that he had an account of such child being among the Mohawks, and determined to go after his child last Fall, but has hitherto been prevented by reason of sickness and deaths in his family. And the loss he hath been at in searching for said child hath been so great, being about one hundred pounds lawful money, that he is not able to bear it, being in a new plantation; and as there is within sixty rods of his door some Province land lying on ye Watchusetts hill, which would be some advantage to him, providing he could have it; therefore, your petitioner humbly prays this Honorable Court to take his case in your compassionate consideration, and make him a grant of ye easterly half of said Wachusett hill."

The only record I find in regard to this petition is the indorsement "negatived," in the handwriting of the Secretary. It is interesting, however, as the father's account of the searches for his lost daughter. The probabilities are this child perished in the woods or pond.

The settlements subsequent to 1751, must have been rapid. The next in time was that of Oliver Davis, upon Clark Hill, near the present line of Hubbardston. Mr. Davis was a man of enterprise, as well as mechanical skill, and having purchased a tract of one thousand acres, partly in this town and partly in Hubbardston, he built the first saw and grist mill in this immediate region, near where the Valley Village Mills now stand.

In June, 1758, there were thirty families in town, as appears by the petition of Benjamin Houghton and others, —then presented for an act of incorporation. In addition, there must have been some score or two of hard-handed yeomen, hewing away with might and main at the primeval forest, to get a clearing and a log house, for the blushing helpmeet they instantly thereupon, every one of them, intended to bring behind him, on a pillion, to these sylvan shades and this mountain home. Why, the dullest ear in the woods could have detected every man chopping under these tender circumstances, by the quicker stroke and merrier ring of his axe, or the smarter or more fantastic whistle following each crash that took one from the obstacles between him and his happiness, while in the distant towns below, hearts watched as anxiously for tidings of "the men about the Watchusetts," as did ever Governor Leverett and his General Court, in the days of "Sagamore Philip, John, Sam, Washaken, Old Queen and Pomhom."

Excellent notions had the sons as well as the fathers, in those days: First freedom; then an axe; then a clearing; then a house; then a wife to make it home; a bible to make it Christian; honest loving labor to give it comfort, and thenceforth every thing went as regular as clockwork, from the care of the dairy to the christening of the children.

That a goodly number of these single men were here, is indicated by the fact that seventy-four names of persons, who represent themselves as "proprietors and inhabitants," appear upon the papers connected with the incorporation, while there were but thirty families.

Many of you may be surprised to learn, that the incorporation was not obtained until after a severe and protracted struggle of more than a year, between the North and South, or in modern language, of quite a sectional character. I have recently found most of the documents which this struggle originated, and they furnish much valuable information in regard to the town at that period.

June 8, 1758, Benjamin Houghton and others, residents of the Farms, and the northerly part of the Wing, presented a petition, praying that "certain farms near the great Watchusetts Hill, and contiguous to Rutland East Wing, containing a track of about six miles by three, together with the East Wing of Rutland, containing about a like quantity, upon which there are about thirty families already settled, be erected into a township." Upon this petition leave was granted to bring in a bill; but nothing more was done until the next session, in January 1759. A petition was then presented by Eliphalet Howe and others, inhabitants of the East Wing, praying that the Wing alone, might be made a town. Upon this petition the Council ordered notice, but the House summarily dismissed it, and with it the previous one of Houghton.

The succeeding February, Houghton and others again petitioned, setting forth " that said farms and Wing being incorporated into a Distinct Township, will make a very good one, and do not contain the contents of six miles square, and that said Wing, by itself, will not be able to defray the charges of building a meeting-house, settling a minister, and maintaining the Gospel among them, and making roads, without an intolerable heavy tax ;" that the farms are not able alone to meet such charges, and " cannot be accommodated to any other town, and will be forever disobliged if not laid to said wing, and both together will find the charges of a new settlement heavy enough ;" that " both wing and farms are at present under very difficult circumstances, by the extreme distance and badness of the roads to the public Worship of God in any other Town." They add, "we can but seldom attend it, and in the winter season are quite shut up, which circumstances are not only distressing to the present Inhabitants, but very Discouraging to new Settlers. Wherefore, the humble prayer of your petitioners is, that said wing and farms may be incorporated as above-said." .

This petition was signed by forty-five persons, of whom twenty-four resided upon "The Farms," and twenty-one upon the "Wing."

Notice was ordered by the General Court, to be given "to the Proprietors and Inhabitants of the East Wing of Rutland," by inserting the substance of the petition in some one of the Boston Newspapers, to show cause if any they had, at the next session of the court, why the prayer of the petition should not be granted.

The notice given was defective in form, and Eliphalet Howe and others, by memorial, took advantage of this. The petition was thereupon postponed to the May session, and new notice ordered and given.

At this session, Joseph Eveleth and twenty-one others, "Inhabitants and Proprietors of the East Wing of Rutland," sent in a long memorial, "in answer to the petition" of Houghton and others, and praying "that said wing might be incorporated into a Town or District." In this they say, "your memorialists beg leave to say, that they are very sure that Every Impartial man that is acquainted with the Situation and Circumstances of said Wing and farms will Readily say that the wing of itself, will make a much better settlement than if the farms are laid to said wing, for this Reason, Because the farms in General, are some of the poorest land, perhaps, that there is in the Province, Lyes in a very bad form, and although the said Proprietors and Inhabitants of said farms, did exhibit a plan to your Excellency and Honors, that appeared that said farms lay in a very good form to be adjoyned to said Wing. Your memorialists beg leave to say, that they are very sure that said plan is not true,—But done, as they apprehend, to Deceive your Excellency and Honors, and as almost all the Best of the land in said wing, Lyes on the Southerly side of it, and the Chief of the Inhabitants living on that Side;

32

and not only so, but the land on the northerly side Never will admit of Half so good a Settlement as the Southerly side will; and if the farms should be annexed to said wing, it would Cary the Center of the wing and farms to the very Northerly side of said Wing, which would oblige the two-thirds of the Inhabitants always to travel Three or Four miles to meeting, and the great Difficulty that your memorialists must be put to in making Highways and Building Bridges through a very Rough, Rocky Country, will Burden them so, that they had rather have one-quarter of their Real estate Taken from them, than to be obliged to Joyne with those People, where they are certain they shall always live in Trouble and Difficulty. And as the said wing contains better than twelve thousand acres of Land, and is capable of making a very good Settlement of itself, and cost your memorialists a very great price; and if your Excellency and Honors should annex the Farms to the wing, we apprehend it would be taking away the Rights of your memorialists, and giving it to those that have no just claim to it." They therefore pray that the petition of Houghton and others may be dismissed, and that the wing may be incorporated into a Town or District.

This petition and memorial was referred to a Joint Committee of the General Court, who gave the parties a hearing, and reported, "That in order to have a clear understanding of the sundry things mentioned in said Petition, that a Committee be appointed and sent by this Honorable Court to view the Farms and the East Wing above mentioned, and Report to the Court, the charge of said Committee to be borne as this Honorable Court shall hereafter order." This Report was accepted, and Gamaliel Bradford, Mr. Witt, and Colonel Gerrish were appointed the Joint Committee.

This Committee had a view and further hearings, and there are sundry papers on file presented to them. Among these are the two following of some interest to us:

"October ye 6th, 1759.—This may certifie whomsoever it may Concern, that the Land Between Leominster, Leuningburg and Narrowgassett No. 2, and as far as the Potash Farm, is Chiefly uninhabitable, and very bad land, and no waye fit but for a very few Inhabitants.

Test our hands :

EZRA HOUGHTON,
JONATHAN WILDER.

LANCESTER, October 7th, 1759.
These may certifie that the Lands north of the farm Called Potash Farm, betwixt Leominster and Narragansett, is Generally Rough Land, and will admit of but few Good Settlements.   Atts :

JOSEPH WILDER,
JOHN BENNIT.
N. B.—The above subscribers were the gentlemen that layed out the above-mentioned Lands and assisted in Dividing them.''

I apprehend much of this controversy turned upon the so often vexing question to towns of the centre.

The final result was, that on the 20th of October, one hundred years ago, the act which occasions our festivities, received the consent of the Royal Governor, and incorporated the town with precisely the same bounds asked for by Houghton and others, and according to the plan presented by them. Looking back through all this period, over our history, not one here doubts, that in putting these two sections together in a well-shaped and substantial town, the law makers did wisely and happily. The fears of the southern section, that if joined to the north they should " always live in trouble and difficulty," and which led them in the heat of controversy to say, that they "had rather have one-quarter of their real estate taken from them than be obliged" to do so, were speedily dissipated. From that day to this, never has a town been more free from sectional strife or division. Were you now to propose to separate the two original divisions, if any mortal man could find the line, you would stir up a thousand fold deeper, more protracted, and bitter struggle than that which brought them together. If there be one common feeling of joy to-day, it is that we are citizens of a common town. And I trust we mean to remain so, as long as Wachusett, our common inheritance, looks down upon a town at all.

The act of 1759 made the territory, in name, a district; but in its own language, invested it "with all the privileges, powers and immunities that towns in the Province did, or might enjoy, that of sending a Representative to the General Assembly only excepted." They had a right to send an *agent* to the General Court, a right which they soon after exercised.

Early in the history of Rutland East Wing, the Rev. Thomas Prince, colleague pastor of the old South Church, Boston, became a large proprietor, owning five of the thirty-three shares. His interest was, probably, at a later period, larger. For this reason, and in respect to him, possibly to smooth matters a little with the Rutland opposition, the town was named Prince Town, a name which the act of 1771 contracted to Princeton.

The first town meeting was held, and the town organized by the choice of the necessary officers, on the 24th of December, 1759. This meeting was at the tavern of Abijah Moore, where all subsequent ones were held, until the meeting-house was boarded and partially finished, in May, 1763. The records of the first meetings are gone from the record book, but it appears, from documents, that Dr. Zachariah Harvey was the first Town Clerk. At this time he occupied, I judge, the most prominent and influential position in town. The petition for incorporation is in his hand-writing. He had come here, not long before, from that part of Shrewsbury then called the Leg, and which lies along our eastern border, now a part of Sterling, and resided on the farm more recently owned and occupied by Deacon Ebenezer Parker.

The first town meeting of which a record exists, was in March, 1761. Dr. Harvey was chosen Moderator, District Clerk, Chairman of the Selectmen, Chairman of the Assessors, and Agent to the General Court, a plurality of offices, I think, never since held by one person. There seems to have been no little trouble and commotion at this meeting, more, by much, I apprehend, than has ever occurred at any of its successors. There is a protest upon the records, signed by eight persons, declaring the proceedings illegal, "by reason of the meeting not being purged from such persons, or voters, as are unqualified by law to vote."

But the matter did not end here. The same March, a long memorial was sent to the General Court, by these and other persons, setting forth that there were, at this meeting, "several votes and transactions altogether illegal and unwarrantable, and unfairly and unduly obtained by means of many persons being admitted to vote at said meeting, that were not legal voters there, and some that were not even inhabitants of the same." They go on, in very plain terms, to charge the Doctor with pretty high-handed and rather awkward measures, and ask to have the proceedings declared void, and another meeting called and new officers chosen.

The Doctor was called upon by the General Court, "to render an account of the proceedings complained of." He filed his answer, which is missing, so that we loose his version of the matter. The decision was in his favor, and the proceedings of the meeting were ratified and confirmed.

At the incorporation, few roads existed. The first of which I can find any trace, was, I suppose, a Province road, from Lancaster to Sunderland. There is a map of it in the State archives. It ran along the north-east line of the town, crossing the edge of Wachusett pond, in Westminster. The distance by it, as stated on the plan, from Lancaster meeting-house to Wachusett pond, is eleven miles. This road was in existence as early as 1735, when a grant of land was made to Samuel Kneeland, on each side of it and near the pond.

The road, I think, also existed through town to Hubbardston. The first road, apparently, built by the town, was that from Westminster line by Mr. John P. Rice's, over

Meeting-House Hill to Holden. This was in 1762. Upon a map of the town, taken as late as 1793, and filed with the Secretary of State, there are laid down only these three roads. Probably most of the early roads were made by a tax, "worked out" upon them, as they have been repaired ever since.

Originally, towns were incorporated, as a general rule, whenever the territory could support a gospel ministry. Hence, the representations in this respect, in the petitions I have cited. This became, therefore, at once the legal duty of the town, and early measures were taken to erect a meeting-house and settle a minister. Instantly there came up this exciting question of the centre, so distressing always in our towns. Several meetings were held upon this trying subject. First, the house was located; then a vote revoking this; then a committee from Bolton, Holden and Westminster, were appointed, with a surveyor from Rutland, and one from Westboro, all to "be under oath for the trust committed to them, to survey the town, find the centre, and affix the place for building the meeting-house on." Of what this sworn committee reported, we unfortunately have no record. The town refused to accept it, and finally voted to locate the house "on the highest part of the land given by John and Caleb Mirick, near three pine trees, marked, being near a large flat rock,"—the site upon Meeting-House Hill, with which they began.

Here, in 1762, the first church was reared, as the record has it, "fifty foots long and forty foots wide."

> " Scarce steal the winds, that sweep his woodland tracks,
> The larch's perfume from the settler's axe,
> Ere, like a vision of the morning air,
> His slight framed steeple marks the house of prayer ;
> Its planks all reeking, and its paint undried ;
> Its rafters sprouting on the shady side.
> It sheds the raindrops from its shingled eaves
> Ere its green brothers once have changed their leaves,—
> Yet faith's pure hymn, beneath its shelter rude,
> Breathes out as sweetly to the tangled wood,

As when the rays thro' blazing oriels pour
On marble shaft and tessellated floor ;
Heaven asks no surplice round the heart that feels,
And all is holy where devotion kneels."

Our fathers were religious men, and long before the building of the meeting-house, maintained religious worship portions of the year, in private dwellings, in different parts of the territory. The first sermon ever preached within our limits was at the tavern of Lieut. Moore, to an audience which a single room held. An old lady living in 1838, told me she remembered hearing a sermon preached there, by Rev. Mr. Harrington, of Lancaster, in 1759, on the occasion of the District's incorporation. " There were then but a handful of us," said she, "who found our way to church by marked trees."

In 1767, the Rev. Mr. Fuller was settled, the first minister of the town. In 1768, upon his petition, in consideration of this, his settlement, with a heavily burdened people, in what he there terms " a wilderness conntry," the General Court granted him Wachusett, and the mountain thus passed to private hands. Mr. Fuller was dismissed at the opening of the Revolution, from difficulties between him and his people, growing out of that great conflict.

I do not propose to trace any history of the town much beyond the point I have reached, and especially I do not the ecclesiastical. Since Mr. Fuller's day, religious controversies have existed, that are happily buried in the past. I have the charity to believe, what it is but justice I should say, that they have all originated in deep convictions of truth, and a sincere and earnest desire to promote it. Sometimes, perhaps, the differences have been greater in appearance than in reality. Parties starting, like the streams from our mountain, have for a time followed in opposite courses, only to find themsleves at last in a common ocean. To-day, at least, we look back on all these scenes, as the sun looks on the sea, to draw up thence all that is pure, and sweet, and invigorating, while it leaves all that is salt and bitter behind. We are not the less attached, as townsmen, because the love of a common Savior constraineth us, in his service, to adopt different denominational forms or creeds.

In 1771, an additional act was passed, by which the gore, of three thousand acres, known in after years as No-Town, was annexed to the town. To this addition the town objected, and the next year petitioned the General Court, setting forth that this was a "strip of land extending a great way from the centre, where the meeting-house stands, and that the inhabitants were poor and unable to make roads, and praying it may be set off again." Upon this petition, in 1773, an act was passed, setting off from the town all the lands which did not belong to the district; so that the limits of the town became precisely the same under the acts of 1771 and 1773, that they were in 1759. Not a foot was permanently added. The map filed in 1793, is identical with the plan of 1759. The only additions since made are five hundred acres from Hubbardston, in 1810, and a like area from No-Town, in 1838. None has been taken off, so that the present area is about twenty thousand acres.

Of the history subsequent to the act of 1771, I have no time to speak in detail. From that period to the present, as already observed, the changes peculiar to the town and distinct from those resulting merely from participation in the general progress, have been less than in most towns. It was, and still is, purely an agricultural town. Its population in numbers, has been about the same for half a century. Its growth, prior to that time, was considerable. The venerable historian of Worcester County, in 1793, says: "In little more than thirty years from its incorporation, Princeton is become very considerable among the towns of the County. It has surprisingly increased in number and wealth. The finest of beef," he adds, "is fatted here, and vast quantities of butter and cheese produced, and from the appearance of their buildings and farms, we must judge the people are very industrious ; " and he closes a glowing description of the seat of Hon. Moses Gill, thus : " Upon the whole, this seat of Judge Gill, all the agreeable circumstances respecting it being attentively considered, is not paralleled by any in the New England States ; perhaps not by any on this side of the Delaware." The President of Yale College, Dr. Dwight, in 1797, speaks of Princeton as a rich grazing township, and adds, " the houses of the inhabitants, and the appearance of their farms, are sufficient indications of prosperity, and the people are distinguished for industry, sobriety and sound morals." He also speaks of Governor Gill's establishment "as more splendid than any other in the interior of the State ; " and he adds what impresses us with the character of the surrounding country even then, that in attempting to make his way to Rutland, " he came very near being lost for the night."

In 1771, there were in town ninety-one dwelling-houses, while in 1790 there were one hundred and forty-four. At the former period there were but one hundred eighty-three and three-fourths acres of tillage land out of the whole twenty thousand, and but one thousand and eighty-three of pasture. But little more than one-twentieth of the land had been subdued, and but a mere fraction brought into cultivation.

There is one other fact revealed by the valuation of 1771, on file at the Capitol, which may astonish some who hear me, and which makes a heaven-wide difference between those days and ours. There was upon these mountain heights, now all vocal with shouts of freedom for the oppressed, and denunciation upon the oppressor, then owned and dwelling, a *slave*—one of the few in the Province. Slavery has existed at the base of Wachusett. The slave's foot has pressed our soil, and the shackles did not fall.

The number of dwelling-houses here in 1800 were but four more than in 1790, while the population in 1810 had increased only forty-six over that of 1790, and probably at this moment, after nearly seventy years, does not exceed it by more than two hundred. Nor has the character of the people changed. Sons have succeeded fathers on the old homesteads, and worthily maintained the family name and honor. Were it not a little out of taste in their presence, I should add, were the historian of Worcester County, or the President of Yale again to pass this way, they would transfer to the sons the language applied to the fathers.

Perhaps the most marked change of the century, or even the last fifty years, is the disappearance of the forest. One returning here to-day, after a quarter of a century's absence, will miss first and most the immense tracts of primeval wood-land he used to see. Next to this absence, he will note a new presence, that of hundreds, of late years, resorting here in the Summer season. The forests have gone, and the fashionables have come. And although every gipsy hat and fluttering ribbon along our highways, from June to September, is a sweet exotic, we would not spare, we cannot help an occasional regret, that the axe has carried its warfare so unrelentingly, and that the woodman has not here and there spared a tree, a remembrance of days lang syne, and a blessing and a beauty for days to come.

When I speak of slight changes, I mean, as I have said, those special and peculiar to the town. In those that have come from the stupendous progress of the century and the country, it has shared to the full measure of the towns in the Commonwealth. Our fathers, from the days when they served under a King, to those when, in town meeting, they could arraign a President, have gone along in full sympathy with every great and good movement around them. Pioneers, they opened the forest, and planted civilization in its depths. They made roads, and built churches. They subdued lands, and reared school-houses. Not in advance of, but never behind, their fellow citizens, they shrank from no duty. From the first gathering of their children to be taught in a private school, to the voting of the last dollar for schooling, they maintained their educational institutions, as you have maintained yours, up to the standard of the State. They and we settled ministers, and they became unsettled, and singularly, not one in the whole century, in any denomination, has died in the occupancy of a pulpit. And yet, what adds to the singularity, but just one has been involuntarily dismissed, and each has held his place up to the average ministerial tenure of his time and denomination. The fathers and the sons, in matters ecclesiastical, have had their divisions and their controversies, sometimes the outbreak of a pervading change in the community, sometimes special to themselves; but they have never failed to give the institutions of the gospel an open, earnest and unwavering support, from the day, uniting all in the doctrines of the great Genevan reformer, they gave Mr. Goodrich a call, to that when the conscientious sympathies of some led them to prefer to the elder faith. the communion of that great church Wesley founded, Whitfield honored, and good men everywhere respect and love.

In all the great struggles that have wrought out and distinguished our country's history, the people of our town have been intelligent, early and active participants. They fought the preparatory battles of freedom with their King against the French, and they fought its actual battles with the French against their King. Their records show them to have been early, constant and discriminating supporters of all the measures of the Revolution, from its faint rising to its glorious consummation. On two occasions, at least, their action was of character and importance enough to secure honorable mention by the latest and ablest of the historians of the United States. The features of numbers of revolutionary pensioners are too distinctly impressed upon our memories to require the details of services in this war.

They voted for our State Constitution. With a love for State sovereignty too ardent to leave the judgment clear and perfect, they opposed the Constitution of the United States when proposed. With a patriotism too large and

6

judicious to yield right to consistency, when adopted they supported and sustained it.

Prior to this, many of them sympathized, and some joined in "Shay's rebellion," and one, if the truth must out, came nearer being hanged than I hope any one else from the town ever will for a like or any cause.

But I must pause. Our Thanksgiving has other services, which exhausted nature already reminds us we are under solemn obligations to perform. If I began while the dinner was cooking, I am continuing while it is waiting. Let me incur no such weighty responsibility.

We have come up here from our homes and occupations, to revive associations, to renew acquaintances, to promote kindly feelings, to strengthen affections, brighten sympathies, and draw tighter the cords of love that bind us to the old family home and fireside.

> The past and present here unite
> Beneath time's flowing tide,
> Like footprints hidden by a brook,
> But seen on either side.

As I have sketched the days long gone, and sought to

> " Review the scenes,
> And summon from the shadowy past
> The forms that once have been,"

I have only followed the necessities of the occasion, and hope my rude and homely attempt may draw some charm from it.

And now, as we look upon what our eyes behold; upon these free hills and valleys, robed in the resplendent beauties of Autumn; upon these farms, from which the teeming harvests have just been gathered and garnered; upon these houses of comfort and plenty; these homes of contentment and love; these churches, reared for the service of God, and these schools for the education of man; upon this prosperous, moral and happy people; and then upon the Commonwealth and common Country, that hold over it the shield of their power and protection, we bend in grateful homage before the Divine author of it all, exclaiming, " surely, the lines have fallen to us in pleasant places, and we have a goodly heritage."

But this anniversary has its lesson. As we stand scanning others, so others, hereafter, will stand to scan us. While we are relating the past of municipal history, we are making the present.

> For the structure that we raise
> Time is with materials filled ;
> Our to-days and yesterdays
> Are the blocks with which we build.
>
> Truly shape and fashion these,
> Leave no yawning gaps between ;
> Think not, because no man sees,
> Such things will remain unseen.
>
> Build to-day, then, strong and sure,
> With a firm and ample base, ·
> And ascending and secure
> Shall to-morrow find its place.

PROGRESS;

A POEM.

BY ERASTUS EVERETT, A. M.,

OF BROOKLYN, N. Y.

The annual bells have rung their hundredth chime
Since thou, O! Princeton, wast ushered into time.
All hail, old Princeton! To childhood's earliest home
Thy noble sons and virtuous daughters come.
From where yon lake reflects the forests green,
In whose pure depths the mirrored hills are seen,
[1] From where young Nashua's silver fountain flows,
[2] Or where Pine Hill his lengthened shadow throws,
From where thy Boylston's princely villa lies,
Or Brook's fields salute the eastern skies,
[3] Where dwelt thy Gill in magisterial state,
And taught thy sons what virtues make us great
From where thy churches' modest spires ascend,
And warn us all to seek in Heaven a friend;
Come from thy utmost borders, here we stand
And, brethren all, each grasps a brother's hand.
A few have roved in distant lands away
From where their infant eyes first saw the day,—
To Hampshire's mountains clad in ice and snow,
To western wilds where lurks the savage foe,
To southern lands where glows a burning sky
And sugared fruits in wild profusion lie.
And they too bid thee hail! They too are come,
Thy truant sons and daughters, welcomed home,
From prairie, hill and vale assembled here
To celebrate with thee thy Hundredth Year.
   Though winds blow fierce from many a woody steep,
And wintry storms their boisterous revels keep,
Though late the snow doth in the furrow lie

4 And dwarfish Fall-flowers prematurely die,
O'er this loved spot affections linger still
And fondly cluster round Wachusett Hill.

PROGRESS I sing :—my muse assist the lay,—
Allied the theme to this auspicious day.
A time there was, when all the vast domain
Of hill and valley, woodland, lake and plain,
From where Katahdin rears his awful head,
(By him Penobscot's gelid springs are fed)
To modern Ophir, California's strand,
Whose rivers flow in beds of golden sand,
From where the wind-god rules the stormy North
And clothes in icy mail the frozen earth,
To where the groves in living green appear
And Spring and Summer share the equal year,—
When all this land so fruitful and so fair,
Alike the patriot's pride and patriot's care,
Was one vast haunt of savage beasts of prey
And Indian warriors fiercer still than they,
Algonquins and Iroquois of various name
Roamed far and wide and chased the antlered game.
Rude Art had taught to bend the supple yew,—
From birchen bark to form the light canoe ;
With that they learned the furry bear to slay ;
With this from lakes to tempt the finny prey.
All this they took as Nature freely gave
In ignorance content no more to crave.
The kindly earth afforded tuberous roots,
Ceres spontaneous, yielded bearded fruits.
Kind Nature thus supplied the place of Art
And made provision for the grosser part,
But no provision made or care had given
For that which makes us men and heirs of heaven.

5 Nor must we fancy this the golden age,
With which the poets fill the mythic page,
When acorns were the simple shepherd's food
And blissful ignorance taught him naught but good.
The savage bosom heaved with passions dire,
With malice, hate, revenge and deadly ire.
Nor men in arms alone the foe engaged :
'Gainst age and sex the fiendish warfare raged.
The hoary sire that in his arm-chair dozed,
The tender babe that in its crib reposed,
Matron and maid in mingled slaughter bled
And swelled the list of prematurely dead.

The captive little cause of joy they gave,
Doomed to a life more dreadful than the grave.
Dire was his punishment: for who can tell
The tortures practised by these hounds of hell!
Not Nero's hate or Herod's jealous rage,
Which stain with blood the classic Gibbon's page,
Not Britain's Queen whose frequent fagots, burned
Round Smithfield's stake, her "Bloody" title earned,
Where Ridley, Latimer and Cranmer bled,
Immortal trio of the martyred dead,
Contrived the tortures ingeniously severe
Which in our early Indian wars appear.

Nor then, loved Princeton, was thy rude domain,
Where Peace, Content and Industry now reign,
Free from the savage foe that nightly prowled
More fierce than famished wolves that round him howled.
On th' eastern slope whence old Wachusett swells,
6 A little girl (for so tradition tells)
Had strayed from home, what time th' autumnal blast
Had strewn the frozen ground with golden mast
And dapple squirrel's merry bark did tell
The huntsmen where his kindred loved to dwell.
Still lured along by objects strange and wild,
Many such objects lured the simple child,
An Indian's feathered plume she sudden spies
And echo answers to her frantic cries.
Around her head the threatening hatchet gleams
And tears and sobs succeed to childish screams.
The neighbors came from all the country round,
Resolved the little wanderer should be found.
They formed a circle, toward the centre drew,
And gave from time to time the loud halloo.
They searched each bush, nook, thicket, hollow tree,
Where'er, by chance, a little child might be:
Prolonged the search, nor ceased from day to day,
Till the last, lingering hope had died away.
Surmises horrible filled each anxious breast,
Surmises long indulged and then expressed:
She lived—had gone 'mong savage tribes to dwell:—
All else conjecture:—the sequel none could tell.
Some said she waded through Canadian snows
To where St. Laurent's mighty current flows;
Some said she pined, a captive, 'neath the skies
Where Saratoga's healing waters rise,
7 Or hoarse Niagara in thunder roars
And down the abyss the ceaseless torrent pours.
Her stricken father travelled far and near

As rumours various reached his eager ear ;
But rumours vain no certain tidings gave
And he forgot his sorrows in the grave.

When but a child, I heard my mother say
How thou, fair Rowlandson, wast driven away.
Pity and rage by turns my bosom stirred
As I the horrors of thy story heard.
She wandered on with painful steps and slow,
And marked with crimson dye the virgin snow.
Methinks I hear her pray with stifled breath,
" O ! God when wilt thou grant relief in death ? "
The night is darkest just before the day ;
Th' all-seeing One watched o'er her weary way,
Brought help from far his cherished child to save
And granted life to one who asked a grave.
8 Concord's illustrious son the ransom paid
On that high rock where we in childhood played ;
Near Graves' swamp where Frost his father slew—
Half idiot Frost, the dread of all he knew.
Such tales as these which freeze the youthful blood
The ancient annals of our town record.
My soul, turn from them. 'Tis well we change the lay
From this dark race that long hath passed away.
No council fires now shed their fitful flame
Or mothers hush their babes with Philip's name.

Genoa's Pilot launched from Palos' shore,
Through unknown seas his timid followers bore,
On Guanahani's coast his flag unfurled
And gave to Castile's Queen another world.
Cabot came next, Caboto rightly named,
In Venice born—Venice for beauty famed.
Amerigo Vespucci next we see,
Born at fair Florence—Italians all the three.
This last the land admired and filled his page
With fabled splendors of the golden age.
Bright golden fishes in the waters played
And gold-winged warblers flitted through the glade :
The waters flowed in beds of golden sand
And hills of gold o'erlooked the happy land.
The waving palms in living green were dressed,
Whose fruits ran nectar ere the lip had pressed.
Green sunny seas the sunny shores did lave
And Nature furnished more than man could crave.
9 The Tuscan thus filled Europe with his fame
And this vast continent received his name.

De Soto first drank Mississippi's wave
And in its turbid waters found a grave.
All gallant Raleigh's cruel fate bemoaned
Who on the block for fancied crimes atoned.
Hudson saw first Manhattan's azure skies,
Where now a thousand marble mansions rise ;
There sculptured piles the distant prospect bound,
There Mammon's self his favorite seat hath found
And Wall-street stands confessed, his consecrated ground.

But who shall fitly name the Pilgrim band,
That launched their ship from low Batavia's strand,
Ploughed the dark sea, nor feared the stormy flood
Which bore them nearer to their equal God !

  " The breaking waves dashed high
    On a stern and rock-bound coast,
  And the woods against a stormy sky .
    Their giant branches tossed :

  And the heavy night hung dark
    The hills and waters o'er,
  When a band of exiles moored their bark
    On the wild New-England shore.''

Thus Hemans sung sublime and swept the lyre
Divinely wild,—her lips were touched with fire—
And who shall dare, presumptuous, to explore
The upward path which she hath trod before ?
10 Our fathers planted here 'mid ice and snow
A fruitful vine which hath not ceased to grow.
O'er hill and vale it shoots its leafy boughs
And distant nations 'neath its shade repose.

Then first the axe through ancient forests rung,
Forests grown old ere yet blind Homer sung ;
The sturdy woodman, doubling stroke on stroke,
Laid low the towering pine and knotted oak ;
The giant trunks in blackened ruins lay
And purblind monsters, frightened, fled the day ;
Earth's bosom heaved with elemental strife
And teemed with a thousand novel forms of life.
Man o'er th' Atlantic brought the noble steed
Which on Granada's plains was wont to feed,
Taught the proud charger of th' embattled field
To the mild yoke his patient neck to yield,
With daily toil to aid the laboring train

And fit the earth to yield the yellow grain.
11 Such thine, O ! Harrington, which we oft have seen
Where mustering troops moved o'er yon shaven green.
When the shrill clarion rent the crystal sky
To tell the host the mimic fight was nigh,
His burning nostrils wide and streaming mane,
Th' impatient bit which spurned the tightened rein,
12 His neck with thunder clothed and eye of fire,
Left us in doubt if most we should admire
The haughty grace with which the charger trod
Or practised skill with which the master rode.
  Each thrifty farmer with his neighbor vied,
By patient implements the sod was plied ;
Exotic shrubs adorned the gay parterre,
Exotic flowers perfumed the morning air ;
The moss-rose bloomed where once the thorn grew wild
And all the land a flowery garden smiled.

  The mother country a cruel step-dame proved,
Nor loved her children but their tribute loved.
She taxed the luxuries and the wants of life,
She taxed the husband and she taxed the wife ;
Th' imported brandy and the home-brewed malt,
The rich man's spices and the poor man's salt.
She taxed their sugar, (and she taxed their tea
Till Boston Mohawks steeped it in the sea.)
Hills piled on hills at length the mountain form
Whose cloud-capped top forebodes the rising storm.
'Neath such a mountain bound, the Titan strove,
In vain, to move the load imposed by Jove.
So, taxes following taxes, one by one,
Grew mountain loads which made a province groan
With giant throws the mountain heaved at length
And Britain knew the infant giant's strength.
  Where yon proud obelisk stands sentinel
To guard the sacred graves of Bunker's Hill,
13 I used to hear my aged kinsmen say
" Balls flew like hailstones," that eventful day.
They in the bloody conflict bore a part ;
Their country's call had taught the warlike art.
Warren just saw the nation's rising sun,
And, falling, died and deathless laurels won.
The day was lost, and patriots nobly bled
But called for vengeance, trumpet-tongued though dead
Then rose the mighty Chief, for valor known
And skill in war, and prudence all his own.
Biding his time, he fled before his foes

As waves arc driven when the tempest blows.
Sudden he turned—when lo ! his foes dispersed,
As clouds are riven when the thunders burst.
He taught the Briton 'neath his eye to quail
And on the Hessian poured the leaden hail.
On Trenton's plains the red-mouthed cannon blazed,
The hireling wretches routed fled amazed,
And Princeton's glorious day our fallen fortunes raised.
Across the flood th' astounding tidings sped
And hoary monarchs trembled while they read.
Not greater panic seized Bolshazzar's hall
When *mene tekel* was written on the wall.
The thunderbolts of war the hero hurled
And, conquering, the stars and stripes unfurled
Which proudly float aloft o'er every sea
And floating, flap the emblems of the free.
The Stars of light guide up to glory's path,
The Stripes are emblems of the nation's wrath.
We've chosen for our Arms the bird of Jove,
Acknowledged chief of birds that soar above.
The Olive proffers peace where'er it goes,
The Arrows hurl defiance at our foes.
E Pluribus proclaims our vast extent,
Unum, the nature of our Government.
The Shield, our yeomanry, unconquered host,
Is still our buckler and our country's boast.
 We teach no arts but those of peace and love
Brought by the Prince of Peace from heaven above.
Let Louis deluge lands in human blood
And be, self constituted, the scourge of God !
Our mission is to benefit mankind
And, dying, leave a heritage of peace behind.
Of warlike arts let Europeans boast,
We yet have art enough to guard our coast.
E'en if they chance to land, they still shall find
We have some cotton-bales to hide behind.
Let their sharp-shooters come with Minie ball
With our Sharp's shooters we will shoot them all.

 But who shall sing the progress of the State
In all that makes a nation truly great !
The Steam-leviathan holds his steady path,
Reckless of time or tide or tempest's wrath ;
O'er the vast ocean speeds his trackless way
Nor yet reposes in the coast-bound bay ;
He mounts the foaming river to its source
Before he slackens in his onward course ;

And yet no monumental shaft doth rise
To tell the world where Robert Fulton lies.
Railroads, Briareus-like, with hundred hands
Bind thirty States and one in iron bands :
O'er prairie, river, valley, hill and plain
The iron-horse speeds on his clattering train,
Transports the products of a thousand fields
Yet meek submission to his master yields.
Prometheus, when he stole celestial fire
To light man's lifeless clay, provoked Heaven's ire ;
Bound on a rock, condemned, he bled
While on his heart th' insatiate vulture fed.
Ah! mighty Fabulist, thou ill didst know
The spark divine possessed by man below.
The Great Creator made him lord of all—
Animals and elements on this earthly ball.
14 Who taught the stork to wing her annual flight
Taught man to bring her from her airy height.
Our Franklin turned the lightning from its way
And on the kite-string saw it harmless play.
Morse, more presumptuous still, prescribed its path
15 Nor yet for this incensed the heavenly wrath.
Field sent the flash along the ocean bed
And through the deep the royal message sped.
Franklin was born on Boston's rounded height,
Morse first at classic Cambridge saw the light,
Field, Stockbridge proudly claims as all her own,
And Massachusetts claims them every one.

Our childhood's joys, though blotted from the mind
Like stars from heaven, have left a light behind.
Ah! halcyon days, when we went forth to snare
The mottled partridge and the bounding hare,
Squirrels and birds to hunt each 'Lection-day
And every Summer spread the new-mown hay.
In yonder lake, we took the frequent bath
And trapped the muskrat in his furrowed path.
When Winter clothed the earth in snowy fleece
We staid at home and played at fox and geese
Or simple morris (but never cards or dice,)
Then sallied forth to skate upon the ice.
Returned home late, we said our evening prayer,
And soon in sleep forgot each boyish care.
There on the hill, where once a willow stood
Close by the pool where played the gosling brood,
The hoary grandsire whiled old age away,
And pipe and Bible closed each happy day.

The giant clock that clicked behind the door,
16 To fix exactly noon, eleven and four,
The oaken staff with curious dog-like head
The chest of drawers and the low-posted bed,
The gold-bowed spectacles that helped the sight
To read the News and Holy page aright—
These precious heir-looms all, we'll treasure still
And, dying, leave one to each loved child by Will.

Transporting joys! when every Fourth of May
We witnessed all the feats of Training-day.
Oft did the captain chide the raw recruit
Who " left the ranks " for gingerbread or fruit,
17 Laughed at his faults, or deeds of mischief done,
Brandished his sword and showed how fields were won.
Pleased with his men the good man learned to glow;
Forgot their blunders and their mischief too.
Careless their merits or their faults to scan,
He all forgave ere penitence began.
Thus to relieve the soldier was his pride,
And e'en his failings leaned to Virtue's side.
This th' Old Militia.   The " Independent " band,
Was famed for martial glory through the land.
They knew the tactics, (all that their captains knew,)
Both Merriams taught, and Major Dudley too.
The brothers Merriam were of warlike fame,
From warlike lineage too 'tis said they came.
By nature martial both ;—Joseph the Colonel's name ;—
The other, Amos, called from holy seer of old,
Was Captain then, and Deacon now enrolled.
Such troops of late swept o'er Magenta's plain,
Choked up Palæstro's river with the slain
And, while the world looked on in silent awe,
Fixed the proud Hapsburg's bounds and gave him law.
    'Twere vain to tell the Captains of renown,
Or even Colonels, born in this goodly town.
'Twere sheer impertinence again to tell
What Russel eloquent has told so well.
These warlike worthies now have civic grown
Fill posts of trust, of honor and renown,
And wear with equal grace, the oak or laurel crown.
At every party gathering round this hill
One served his party, and he served them well.
He calmed their petty quarrels, hushed their broils,
Professed the creed, " *To victors be the spoils*,"
And he was bidden, as a fit reward,

This goodly Township's correspondence guard.
18 He kept the papers too, nor kept too long
When State elections drew th' annual throng.
Too honest he to fawn or seek for power
By tricks oft practised in the eventful hour.
Scarce did the coachman light from off his box,
When bankers hurried in to learn the price of stocks ;
And many a blushing maiden he made glad
With rhyming ditties from her absent lad,
By gilt-edged letters made completely well
Both pining widow and consumptive belle.
19 The Doctor now prescribes for female ills,
Along with gilt-edged letters, gilded pills.
To him the politicians all resort
For news from Zurich or St. James' court,
Or that last speech the " Little Giant " made,
And " guess" if Wise or Douglas has the wiser head.
Little reck I, assured that both must yield,
And Banks or Seward win the well-fought field.

Ladies, your smiles suggest another theme,
20 Ah ! yes, the very same, 'tis Love's young dream.
O beauteous maidens, how shall I declare
Your charms ? Vain were the task and I forbear.
Consult your mirrors, and you shall almost see
What charming creatures your mothers used to be.
A grace that mocks the Grecian sculptor's art
Beams in the eye and moves in every part,
That witching smile and dimple, faintly show
Your mothers' beauty thirty years ago.

Seven sister stars look down from Taurus' height,
Seven Grecian Sages saw bright wisdom's light,
Seven golden lamps in darkened Asia shone,
21 And thrice seven preachers, Princeton calls her own.
Go forth, ye heralds of the living God !
Cross desert, jungle, valley, hill and flood ;
Proclaim salvation free, unsold, unbought,
And teach the blessed truths the Saviour taught.
Pagan and Jew the great Messiah shall own
And shine as stars in your eternal crown.

As early memories throng around the heart
And later griefs, for each hath had his part,
We heave th' unbidden sigh, an offering given
To absent ones, too early called to heaven.
Three generations,—all have passed away

Within the century we close to-day.
The first had ended this tragi-comic strife
Ere we were ushered upon the stage of life ;
The second only feeble traces left behind
Among the shattered pictures of the mind ;
The third in limb and, feature yet remain,
Entire, unmarred by fracture, blur or stain.

  Pardon, my townsmen, the tribute of a tear
Paid to the one my memory holds most dear.
On the same day, we drew the vital air,
On the same couch forgot each daily care,
At the same notch, we turned the steel-yard beam,
In the same field, we urged the sluggish team ;
In Dartmouth's Halls both sought for wisdom's lore,
Both left, when duty called, our native shore.
We went far off in Southern lands to dwell :—
He died, and half his virtues none can tell.
Oh ! brother, lost one, whither art thou fled ?
Hold'st thou thy nightly vigils by my bed ?
Know'st thou the fancies that possess my brain,
When in my dreams thou seem'st alive again ?
Rejoicest thou before the throne of God
No more to smart beneath Affliction's rod ?
Where'er thou art, in bright angelic spheres,
Or sent to calm thy doubting brother's fears,
To me the world is palled in frequent gloom
For thou art gathered to the mouldering tomb.
Though fortune smile—give all she ever gave,
My life will be a bark on stormy wave.
Lo ! heavenly visions dawn upon my sight,
I see thee clad in robes of living light,
And I rejoice that thou hast won the Christian fight.

NOTES.

(1) page 44.
" From where young Nashua's silver fountain flows."

The Nashua has four sources in the town of Princeton, viz : two which rise on the north side of Wachusett mountain and flow into Wachusett Lake ; one which flows through the farm of Mr. Roswell Osgood ; and one which rises between Pine Hill and Wachusett mountain, &c.

(2) page 44.
" Or where Pine Hill his lengthened shadow throws."

Pine Hill is very high and very precipitous, so that there is no mountain of which it can be said so significantly that it throws a " lengthened shadow."

(3) page 44.
" Where dwelt thy Gill in magisterial state."

The late Lieut. Governor Gill, of Massachusetts, dwelt in a mansion which stood not far from the present residence of Dr. Boylston.

(4) page 45.
"Though late the snow doth in the furrow lie."

The snows are more abundant about Wachusett mountain than in any other part of the State, except, perhaps, the Berkshire Hills. This mountain forms the water-shed between the Connecticut and the Merrimack ; it is about 2900 feet in height.

(5) page 45.

The follies of the golden age were revived by Jean Jacques Rousseau, who, in his Essay before the Academy of Dijon, maintained that virtue can be found among the ignorant only, and that vice is a necessary accompaniment of education.

(6) page 46.
" On th' eastern slope whence old Wachusett swells,
A little girl (for so tradition tells.)"

As the fate of the " Lost Child " has always created great interest and sympathy, I have taken great pains to solve the mystery which has hitherto surrounded it. Having, while in Princeton at the time of the Centennial Celebration, seen a letter, written by Mrs. Cornelia B. K. Brown, dated at Eaton, New York, in 1827, which gave the death-bed confession of a man who declared that he had murdered the child, I determined to get further particulars, if possible, and wrote Mrs. Brown, scarcely hoping to receive an answer. I was agreeably disappointed by the receipt of a letter, dated "Rockport, Bourbon County, Kansas Territory, Dec. 8th 1859." She says: "I gave more credence to the report from the fact, that all the years of my girlhood were spent within half a mile of Mrs. John Gleason, of Princeton, whose name, previous to her marriage, was Mrs. Patty Keyes, sister to the lost child Lucy, and one of the 'two sisters who went to the pond for sand;' and I have many times listened as she related the sad story of the child's disappearance, together with other incidents that, in my opinion, corroborated the truth of Mrs. Anderson's statement. Mrs. Anderson, of Deerfield, New York, witnessed the confession, told it to Mrs. Whitmore, and she gave it to me. Mrs. Whitmore has been dead more than thirty years. Mrs. Anderson I never saw, and whether she is still living I do not know."

* * * * * * * * *

"I was told that Mr. Littlejohn was thought to be dying for three days. At length he arose in bed, and speaking audibly, said he could not die until he had confessed a murder that he committed many years before. Said he was formerly a neighbor of Robert Keyes, of Princeton, Mass. There was a misunderstanding between the two families. Mr. and Mrs. Keyes felt unpleasantly to live thus, and went to Mr. S's. to effect, if possible, a reconciliation, which having been, apparently, accomplished, and mutual pledges of renewed friendship exchanged, they, Mr. K. and wife, returned home. But the enmity of Mr. S. had not subsided. He sought revenge; and afterwards, seeing the little daughter alone in the woods, to avenge himself on the parents, killed her by beating her head against a log, and then placed her body in a hollow log and went to his house. When the neighbors were solicited to assist in searching for the lost, he was among the first, and being familiar with the forest, he volunteered to lead the party, carefully avoiding the hollow lóg, till night. After dark he went to the hollow log, took the body and deposited it in a hole, which had been made by the overturning of a tree."

Littlejohn died at Deerfield, New York. The date of his death is all that remains to be learned. This bad man lived on the place now owned by Ephraim Osgood. I have other letters, one from the Town Clerk of Deerfield, and one from Rev. Samuel Everett, of Iowa City, whose wife is a niece of the lost child, both tending to confirm the statements of Mrs. B. The interest of the subject is my only apology for having been thus minute. I have only to add that the mother was brought to the verge of insanity by the loss of her little girl, and for a long time after her disappearance, she always went out at night-fall and called, Lu–cy! but the echo from the aged forests was the only answer.

(7) page 46.

"Or hoarse Niagara in thunder roars."

The word *Niagara*, signifies in the Iroquois language, *the thunder of the waters.*

(8) page 47.

*"Concord's illustrious son the ransom paid
On that high rock where we in childhood played."*

Mrs. Rowlandson was taken prisoner at the burning of Lancester, Feb. 10th, 1765, and after wandering about with her savage masters for several months, probably till November, she was redeemed by Captain Hoar of Concord. Tradition has fixed the place of her redemption on the high rock known as the Rowlandson Rock, situated in Everettville, Princeton, Mass. On this rock I have spent many a happy hour. Hon. Edward Everett, (Mount Vernon Papers, Nov. 19th, 1859,) says: "The captivity of Mrs. Rowlandson is not to be read without tears, after a lapse of nearly two centuries."

(9) page 47.

"The Tuscan thus filled Europe with his fame,
And this vast continent received his name."

In Irving's life and voyages of Columbus, Putnam's Edition, 1849, Vol.
III, page 343, I find the following:

"Note to the Revised Edition, 1848.—Humboldt, in his Examen Critique,
published in Paris, in 1837, says: 'I have been so happy as to discover,
very recently, the name and the literary relations of the mysterious
personage, who (in 1507), was the first to propose the name of America,
to designate the new continent, and who concealed himself under the
Grecianized name, Hylasomylas.' He then, by a long and ingenious
investigation, shows that the real name of this personage was Martin
Waldseemuller, of Fryburg, an eminent cosmographer, patronized by
Riene, Duke of Loraine, who, no doubt, put in his hands the letter
received by him from Amerigo Vespucci. The geographical works of
Waldseemuller, under the assumed name of Hylasomylas, had a wide
circulation, went through repeated editions, and propagated the use of
the name America throughout the world. There is no reason to suppose
that this application of the name was in any wise suggested by Amerigo
Vespucci. It appears to have been entirely gratuitous on the part of
Waldseemuller."

It is peculiarly gratifying to be able to settle this question by an
appeal to the Historian, whose death has recently cast a gloom over
Sunnyside, but whose writings his countrymen will not willingly let die.

(10) page 48.

"Such thine, O! Harrington, which we oft have seen."

The late Captain Harrington of Princeton is here referred to. He was
very proud of his horse which was, indeed, one of the noblest specimens of
that noble animal. Persons who used to attend the musters at Lancaster
thirty-five years ago will recognize the picture.

(11) page 49,

" Our fathers planted here 'mid ice and snow
A fruitful vine which hath not ceased to grow."

Ps. LXXX, 10—11.—The hills were covered with the shadow of it, and
the boughs thereof were like the goodly cedars.
She sent out her boughs unto the sea, and her branches unto the rivers.

(12) page 49.

"His neck with thunder clothed, and eye of fire."

Job XXXIX, 19.—Hast thou clothed his neck with thunder?

(13) page 49.

"I used to hear my aged kinsmen say
Balls fell like hailstones that eventful day."

The kinsmen here referred to are my maternal uncle, Abijah Wood, late
of Westminster, who was at the battle of Bunker's Hill, and my grandfather, the late Joshua Everett, who held a Lieutenant's commission during
the Revolution, and made a campaign in the Jerseys.

58

(14) page 51.

"Who taught the stork to wing her annual flight."

JER. VIII, 7.—Yea, the stork in the heaven knoweth her appointed times ; and the turtle, and the crane, and the swallow observe the time of their coming.

(15) page 51.

"Nor yet for this incensed the heavenly wrath."

For a long time after the invention of the lightning rod, by Dr. Franklin, its introduction was opposed on the ground that it was presumption to avert, in this manner, the judgments of God.

(16) page 52.

"To fix exactly noon, eleven and four."

Noon was the hour of dinner. At eleven and four our ancestors were in the habit of taking the semi-diurnal dram. This was before the organization of Temperance Societies and a little *New England* was thought necessary for frequent infirmities.

(17) page 52.

"Laughed at his faults, or deeds of mischief done,
Brandished his sword and showed how fields were won.
Pleased with his men, the good man learned to glow,
Forgot their blunders and their mischief too ;
Careless their merits or their faults to scan,
He all forgave ere penitence began.
Thus to relieve the soldier was his pride,
And e'en his failings leaned to Virtue's side."

Imitated from Goldsmith :

Wept e'er his wounds, or tales of sorrow done,
Shouldered his crutch and showed how fields were won.
Pleased with his guests, the good man learned to glow,
And quite forgot their vices in their woe ;
Careless their merits or their faults to scan,
His pity gave ere charity began.
Thus to relieve the wretched was his pride,
And e'en his failings leaned to Virtue's side.

(18) page 53.

"He kept the papers too, nor kept too long."

One of the tricks of " the party," is to keep back papers which contain news of defeats elsewhere, on the eve of an election, so that the voters may not be influenced by the news.

(19) page 53.

"The Doctor now prescribes for female ills."

Doctor Brooks succeeded Colonel Gill as postmaster, but a few months before the reading of this poem.

59

(20) page 53.

"Ah! yes, the very same, 'tis Love's young dream."

"————genitoris imagine capta."—Virgil.

(21) page 53.

"And thrice seven preachers Princeton calls her own."

It is thought that Princeton may challenge comparison with any other town of the same population, for the number of Ministers of the Gospel that have been born within its limits. With a population of less than one thousand four hundred, it has given birth to twenty-one clergymen. Their names, arranged pretty nearly with reference to seniority, are as follows :

Rev. Sylvanus Haynes,
" Abel Woods,
" Leonard Woods, D. D.,
" Thomas Mason,
" William Mason,
" Charles Brooks,
" John Keyes,
" Humphrey Moore, D. D.
" Samuel Everett,
" Joshua Eveleth,
" Ephraim Eveleth,

Rev. Oliver Allen, D. D.,
" Elisha Perry,
" Ebenezer Mirick,
" Moses Gill,
" William Allen,
" Ezra Newton,
" William P Smith,
" W. W. Parker,
" William Phillips,
" Joel Gleason.

Rev. Oliver Allen, D. D , late Missionary to Bombay, " Princeton calls her own," as his parents moved from Barre, where he was born, to Princeton, when he was only five years old, and he resided here constantly afterwards.

The Morning Session closed with the singing of an original Hymn, written by Rev. William T. Briggs, Pastor of the Church in which the services were held, in the tune of Old Hundred.

HYMN.

Here, where our fathers stood, we stand,
The confluence of a mighty stream ;
And voices from the far off land,
Blend with the day, the hour, the theme.

A century past!   A century hence !
To-day the nuptial knot we tie ;
We link them in the noblest sense,
With thoughts and deeds which cannot die.

By all the memories of this hour—
By yonder graves where sleep our sires,
By these grand hills whose summits tower
High o'er this altar's kindling fires ;—

By all the gleanings of the past ;
By sacred earth, and skies o'erhead ;
Here let us vow—while life shall last,
To emulate the pious dead.

And when we sleep beneath the sod,
Where fathers and where mothers lie—
Come thou blest Savior—mighty God !
And bear us all to realms on high.

Benediction, by Rev. John Goodwin.

THE DINNER.

The Procession, escorted by the Band, reached the tent, where an abundant dinner had been prepared by Capt. Fletcher, of Leominster, at about two o'clock.

When the large company, numbering more than a thousand persons, had taken their seats, the President of the day said:

Ladies and Gentlemen:—Our fathers, we trust, acknowledged God in all their ways. As we are about to partake of the fruits of His bounty, the Divine Blessing will be asked by Rev. Dr. Allen.

Prayer was accordingly offered by Dr. Allen.

In consequence of the state of the weather, which was blustering and cold, it was judged prudent to return, after the close of the dinner, to the Church, that the sentiments and addresses which were anticipated, might be given there.

AFTERNOON SERVICES IN THE CHURCH.

When the company had again taken their places in the Church, which was well filled, the President rose, and having called the assembly to order, said:

Ladies and Gentlemen:—Assembled as we have been to-day, to celebrate the hundredth anniversary of the incorporation of the Town of Princeton, it becomes my pleasant duty, on this occasion, to extend to you a welcome.

Had we met here, ladies and gentlemen, to partake of the repast, which now is among the things that are missing, and must be remembered with those that are gone by; had we assembled to interchange social congratulations, the day, the occasion would have been worthy of such a gathering. But we meet to-day, ladies and gentlemen, for a higher and more noble purpose. We come here, I trust, first of all, with our hearts full of gratitude to the Author of all good, and who governs the destinies of nations as well as of individuals, for His great mercy and goodness to our fathers in their time of toil and labor. They established the institutions which we to-day so richly enjoy. We come here to commemorate the deeds and the acts of our fathers.

But, ladies and gentlemen, I will not detain you a moment. The speaking for this day and occasion, has been assigned to other and abler minds. Permit me then, sons and daughters of Princeton; those who have been absent but have now returned; adopted sons and daughters; strangers who have honored us with your presence on this occasion; male and female, young and old, rich and poor; one and all, we bid you a hearty, cordial welcome.

We will now attend to the intellectual feast of the day. The first sentiment will be announced by our Toast-Master, Joshua T. Everett.

No. 1. *The Day we Celebrate*—The close of the first century of our municipal existence. It greets us as freemen; still in the possession and full enjoyment of all those precious rights of man, intended to be secured to us by the founders of the free republican government of the old Bay State. It stirs anew our sympathies for the oppressed. It inspires us with deep thankfulness for the past, high hopes for the future, and fresh resolves to be ever vigilant in the cause of impartial liberty; and affords the cheering augury that the rounding of another such a period of time will find these hills and valleys radiant with the fires of freedom; teeming with an intelligent and virtuous people, peaceful as a gentle Autumn day, and free as the whistling winds that play round our own Wachusett.

The Band played "Hail Columbia," in response to the patriotic sentiment.

No. 2. *The Sons of Princeton*—Our town has reared men of eminence for their genius, their learning, their wisdom, and their wit; but we are able to add to-day one distinguished name MOORE to the number.

THE PRESIDENT—Will our venerable friend Moore supply what *Moore* seems to be needed on this occasion?

REV. HUMPHREY MOORE, D. D., of Milford, New Hampshire, now eighty-one years of age, responded to the call, as follows :

Mr. President and Ladies and Gentlemen :—I thought this was a farming town, and that there were teamsters here, who were used to teaming with oxen. When I was a boy, teamsters put the steers and young oxen forward and the old ones behind. (Laughter.) But you have seemed to reverse the order of custom, if not the order of nature ; you have brought up the old ox here to stand in front, not in the rear. But as you hold to improvement and advancement, and to the reversion of nature and custom, I will say a few words.

I understand from the sentiment read by the Toast-Master, that the sons of Princeton are to be addressed. But where are the daughters? I find them not in the sentiment expressed. But I suppose the sentiment will allow us to infer that the *sons embrace* the daughters. (Laughter.) We will take them both together, then. (Renewed laughter.) Fellow townsmen and women, I am a son, an old son—I will not say an old boy—of Princeton. I am nineteen years and one day younger than Princeton. I have not any distinct recollection of what transpired during those nineteen years, inasmuch as I was not on the soil of Princeton. But, in 1778, between the 18th and 19th of October, one dark night, it is stated by the records of the town, that one by the name of Moore, came into this place. (Laughter.) I don't recollect the fact. (Renewed merriment.) I do not recollect the circumstances, but I believe tradition, and I believe the record. And now, here I stand to make some remarks, which I could wish might prove appropriate.

In referring to my early life, I will say that five young men, before me, from this town, passed through college. They all became Clergymen, men of talents, men of character, and, I believe, men of usefulness in their respective places. Next after them, one Moore came forward for the purpose of preparing for College. He had but little means for the purpose. The first time he ever saw the inside of a school-house, he was between nine and ten years of age. If I speak of my personal history to the extent of an inch in length, half an inch in width, and no depth at all, will you indulge me ? (Go on, go on !)

I attended the District school two months and a half per year, till I was fifteen years of age. With the addition of five months instruction, I was a member of Harvard College. My father died when I was twelve years old. He left me one hundred pounds—not of silver, not of bank bills, but in the currency of the State. When I was fifteen, with what little perquisites I had, I was worth the immense sum of twenty-five dollars, and with that sum I fitted for College. (Applause.) I would say this to boys, if they are here, but for the parents who have boys, that they may apply the remark to the boys.

I graduated at Harvard College some time before I was twenty-one. The first year after I left College, I passed six months teaching school, and five months in a Theological course ; and one month before my year was out, I stood where preachers stand. I did this by labor—intense labor. My mind was fixed on my object, and I went forward with all my might. In 1802, I bolted over the line which separates Massachusetts from New Hampshire, and there I settled in the ministry, and was there a quarter of a century, with a salary of four hundred dollars a year ; and it was but a short time, even then, before the people suspected that I was growing fat, and that I should get too fat if I kept in that course. But, my friends in

Princeton, I lived it through; I am alive yet, and I am here ready to testify to the necessity for, and success of mental labor.

I will say one word respecting Princeton. I think it a place of remarkable stability. The mountains stand as they did; the hills stand as they did; the streams of water run in their former course. There is no change in them. Yes, and Princeton is remarkable for its integrity. The farms are of the same extent and the same shape as they were when I was born. Scarcely a house is put up between a house for eighty years, except in some cases, in the middle of the town. And I can testify in behalf of the town—and when in my own region I have been disposed to compliment the town in which I originated, and myself with the same stroke—that Princeton is the Prince of towns for raising oxen, men, and stone wall. (Applause.)

No. 3. *The Town of Princeton*—Receiving its name from an eminent *minister* of the Gospel, and an earnest advocate of civil and religious liberty, we are assured that her people will in future, as they have in times past, honor his name and character, by their zeal and efforts to extend the blessings of Christianity and liberty to all the human race.

Rev. Dr. ALLEN, for many years a minister in India, responded.

Mr. President, and Ladies and Gentlemen: What we have heard to-day concerning the individual whose name is here mentioned, an eminent minister of the Gospel, appears to render it unnecessary that I should say much concerning him beyond this, that he was one of the most distinguished ministers of the day. He was one of the largest proprietors of this town, and was father-in-law of the most eminent citizen of the town—Governor Gill. We have his likeness here, hanging before us, and we had, this forenoon, a bound volume of his sermons in his own hand-writing, and I understood that there was a printed volume also. So that we see he was an author before the public. He was one, every way, of nature's noblemen, and com-

9

bined a rare assemblage of qualities, as a patriot, a public man, and a minister of the Gospel.

So, Princeton has a noble name; and I may sáy further, that the first generation of people, as we have heard to-day, were noble men, zealous, yea, jealous for their rights, not only for their rights as citizens, but zealous and jealous for their religious rights also.

My memory, although it does not go back so far as that of our venerable friend who has just addressed you, extends back more than half a century, and very distinctly do I recollect things that I saw and heard at that time, and among them many sermons from Dr. Murdock, the minister at that time. I can remember among texts, the division of his subject, and his argument and illustrations very well. Some sermons that he preached in connection with foreign missions, made a deep impression on my mind. I remember them more distinctly than anything I heard from him. He preached a series of sermons on the same subject, in connection with the first enterprise in this country for foreign missions. To carry out that enterprise, a subscription was taken up, and people were astonished at the amount received. This shows how strong a feeling there was among the people. One man said he did not think there was so much money in town, and another did not believe there was so much *left* in town.

This spirit was kept in lively exercise for years, and I grew up under these impressions. And so it is not strange that, after having finished my college and professional course, I felt it my duty to engage in that cause; and thirty-two years ago last Spring, I preached my farewell sermon in the church then on the hill yonder, and took leave of all my friends, as I supposed, for life. In a few days afterwards I embarked for a foreign mission. At that time, such an enterprise was quite a different thing from what it is now, so little was then known of the heathen world. We found India, the country to which we went, very different from what we had anticipated, about as different as to costumes and customs as it was possible for people to be, and yet belong to the human family. But I had gone, as I believed, for a good purpose, and I at once adopted that country as my own, and such continued to be my views and feelings for more than a quarter of a century. India is a magnificent country; with the highest mountains in the world; rivers and plains, scarcely equalled by any in the world, in a higher state of cultivation than is generally supposed; a country full of people, containing a population six times as large as all the United States, and it was probably as populous two thousand years ago as it is now. And what is remarkable is, that that country, for so many years, had continued almost without change in its customs and manners, and in its social and religious institutions.

In the providence of God, my health became so much impaired, that after using all the means I could in that country, I was informed that if I would preserve myself for anything more in life, or live any longer, I must leave that climate. I returned gradually, through Egypt, the western part of Asia, and the eastern and western parts of Europe, going slowly here and there, for the improvement of my health, so that I saw much of those parts of the world and people, who were Heathen, Mahomedan, and believers in different corrupt forms of Christianity.

On returning to this country, I renewed my acquaintances with the people here, and I found them, as I had reason to expect, to be worthy of their parents. During my long absence, those whom I had known in their old age were all gone; those who were then in middle age were, perhaps, half living, but greatly changed; and another generation had grown up, who were *not* when I went away. But I found the people so well informed in respect to all the circle of benevolent efforts, that any person who did not know their parents, and what a strong hold the cause of benevolence had taken here, would have been greatly surprised. Such, I doubt not, is the character of the people now, and such, I trust, it will continue to be for future generations.

Not many years ago, I met a gentlemen, rather an intelligent and well-educated man, who said to me that he had become quite discouraged, that our great benevolent enterprises were proving a failure. Here, said he, the Anti-Slavery cause is likely to prove a failure; then the Temperance cause and other causes were referred to in the same spirit. I told him I had not those desponding views concerning them; that I did not think the creation of the heavens and the earth, which God had pronounced " good," again and again, and of which He had been and is still the governor, had proved to be a failure. I did not think Christianity, which was ushered into the world with the shouts of " glory to God in the highest; on earth peace, and good-will toward men," had proved to be a failure. I did not think it ever would fail; that so far from failing, it would prove the great power to raise men from oppression and sin; that it had done a vast deal of good for the world, and would do much more. I did not think the efforts for liberty which our fathers made, had proved a failure, but that God had great and glorious purposes to accomplish yet by our nation. I am glad to say this gentleman did not belong to Princeton, and I hope none here ever will take such a view of Christianity, or of the state of the world, or of the government of our country, as he did; but that you will all pray as fervently, and strive as earnestly as though all were depending upon you, and yet trust in God as implicitly for his blessing, as if nothing depended on you. Only go on in this spirit, pressing forward and looking upward, and all will be well with you, with your posterity, and with the world. (Applause.)

No. 4. And I will bring thy seed from the east; with spikenard and saffron, calamus and cinnamon; with all the trees of frankincense, myrrh and aloes, with all the chief spices, with the powders of the merchant.

Mr. Everett stated, that it was supposed that this sentiment would be responded to by Dr. MYRON O. ALLEN, of Wenham, a son of the gentlemen who had just spoken, born in India. He was not able to be present, but had sent a letter full of noble sentiments. He would read it.

WENHAM, OCT. 15th, 1859.

J. T. EVERETT, ESQ.:

It is with deep regret that I find myself obliged to decline your kind invitation to attend the Centennial Celebration of the incorporation of Princeton. I cannot indeed claim it as my birth-place ; but as the residence of my ancestors, and the home of my early years, I shall always feel a deep and filial interest in the good old town. Its grand old hills, swept by the storms of centuries, have impressed their forms upon my mind with all the vividness of reality. Wachusett, Sugar Loaf, the lesser Wachusett, the old Meeting-House Hill,—I can see them yet, as vividly as if gazing from their bald and cloud-capped summits.

Nor are the natural features of the place its only attractions. Those rugged hills have reared a race of men of clear heads and warm hearts, as well as of stalwart forms. Their kindness to me, a stranger and an orphan. will not soon be forgotten.

The township is the foundation stone of all our free institutions. These independent municipal corporations were, from their origin, republics in miniature. Their meeting—scenes, as they often were, of earnest contention and even wrangling—were schools of republicanism. In them were trained the men who made laws, and erected the superstructure of our State and national institutions. Whoever would trace the history of "Liberty in America," must study the history of the towns ; he will find them, in miniature, the history of the nation.

Well, then, may we celebrate the anniversary of our native town. Well may she call back her scattered sons, and there are many of whom she may be justly proud—they are her priceless jewels. Wisely may we meditate the stern virtues of our fathers—their example is our noblest inheritance.

As you request a sentiment, I will venture to offer the following :

The good old Town of Princeton—May she in the future, as in the past, be the nursery of men solid as her granite rocks, pure as her mountain rills, aspiring like her lofty hills, from the low cares and pleasures of earth to the atmosphere of heaven. The hills of the sunny South, the broad prairies of the West, the "coral strands" of India, and the distant isles of the ocean rise and call her blessed.

With sentiments of much respect, truly yours,

MYRON O. ALLEN.

J. T. EVERETT, ESQ., Chairman of Committee on Toasts, &c.

No. 5. *Our Native and Natural Productions*—While time and experience have taught us the great worth of our Fullers, our Woods, our Bangs, Moores, Allens, Russells and Everetts; our Flocks and Herds; our Wheat, Barley and *Corn*, we are yet in doubt as to the real qualities of our *Cobb*.

THE PRÉSIDENT—And we propose, now, to test the quality of the Cobb—not the ordinary cob, ladies and gentlemen, but the *Major Cobb.* (Laughter.)

Thus plainly called for, Major MOSES G. COBB, of Dorchester, a descendant, by one of the branches of the family, from Hon. Moses Gill, whose name he bears, came forward and said:

Mr. President, and Ladies and Gentlemen of Princeton: What a theme the sentiment proposes for research and for thought. The farmers of Princeton can scarcely expect me to enter into a discussion of the merits of Agriculture. You are an agricultural township, as the orator has well said to-day; you are essentially an agricultural town. I can only hope that sooner or later, every State in the Union will have an agricultural department in its executive government, as ours has, and that the national executive will have, as a branch of its fostering care and solicitude, an agricultural department. You, farmers of Princeton, have no cause for reproach in this respect. I believe that you always honored and fostered the science of agriculture. Cattle-Show day, at Worcester, Mr. President, is among the ineffaceable memories of my boyhood. I can, even now, feel the pride with which I used to point out to the boys less fortunate than myself, as I supposed, the beautiful products of Princeton; its handsome cattle, its vegetables, its grains, its almost word-renowned butter and cheese, and if I remember rightly, sir, its good old-fashioned brown bread, made by the housewives and daughters of Princeton, in a large measure, sir, out of that staple of Princeton—Indian corn. But at no time do I remember to have seen exhibited there, any Cobbs. (Laughter.)

I have been aware of the skill, the enterprise, the energy of the Princeton farmers, and the perfection to which they have brought every branch of agriculture, leaving nothing untried which ought to be tried, and trying only those that should be. I am aware, sir, of the increased value, as an article of human diet, both in this country and the old, of Indian corn, the exports having increased in five years—from 1851 to 1857—from one million five hundred thousand bushels, to over seven million five hundred thousand bushels; and the export of Indian meal has increased in the same ratio. But I believe it remained for the Princeton farmers to test the quality of Cobbs. On this matter of Cobbs, I believe I have nothing to be ashamed of in my ancestry. Mr. Samuel Cobb, who was quite an early settler in the south-western part of this town, and who was the progenitor of the Princeton Cobbs, was a worthy, sober, well-to-do farmer, and came here from Cape Cod. I believe all the Cobbs in the country came from that section of the State. I believe all the Cobbs, male and female, have been industrious, honest, sober people, fulfilling the trust imposed upon them; and now and then a Cobb has stood out from the general mass of mankind. I will say no more of the family of Cobbs, except to add, that it is a great source of regret to me that there is no family bearing my name in Princeton.

As for myself, I have come up here to-day,—and I do not know that I shall ever repay the debt of gratitude I owe the citizens of Princeton, who have allowed me to do it,—I have come up to look out upon one of the most beautiful panoramas in the world, almost, the charm of my boyhood, to breathe its pure and bracing air with the companions of my youth; to see the " old folks," and shake them by the hand; and, let me say, they do not appear a day older than when I was a boy.

I feel grateful that my boyhood was in this place, where I could trace my home, by metes and bounds, not by a figure on the wall, or on a door, and I have resolved to-day, that, sooner or later, I shall make my home again in Princeton. (Applause.)

But, sir, another source of sorrow and regret has come over me to-day. My friend, the Orator of the day, really destroyed my dinner by informing me, seriously, that there was a vote passed in 1760, to this effect: That the meeting-house be painted, provided the Hon. Moses Gill will furnish the paint. Now, I am indirectly a descendant of that honorable gentleman. His name has descended to me, but none of his money, and I was alarmed, at first, to think, that this day, and here, that old resolve should be brought forward, and I be called upon to paint the meeting-house. I found out, however, I thought, a way of escape. There is nowhere a resolve that the house *shall* be painted. I also remembered the reply of the Irishman to the farmer, who complained that he had not dug his potatoes as he was expected to do. Said he: "If you want your potatoes dug, fetch 'em along." So I say, if you want your house painted, fetch it down to Boston, and I will see that it is painted. (Laughter.)

Let me give this sentiment in conclusion:

The Farmers of Princeton—The most economical people in the world. They not only know how to raise and shell their corn in the best manner, but they make mince-meat of their Cobbs.

(Great Laughter.)

No. 6. *The Chairmakers of East Princeton*—May they always be of good, substantial timber, free from all the knots and shakes of bad timber and miscalculation. May their backs not be too crooked to permit them to stand erect and boldly against all vice. May thay be shaved and turned to the perfect model of integrity and virtue, and use just enough of the sand-paper of self-denial to smooth off all the rough corners of intemperance, and the use of the weed. May the glue of their friendship and love hold them together, and firmly unite them in the pure bonds of wedlock. May they never be stained with crime, but beautifully painted with the graces of humility and charity, and ornamented with the gold-leaf of Christian benevolence and world-wide philanthropy. In short, in their whole model, manufacture, and finish, may they be done up BROWN. Nye, more! May they be like the faithful Stewarts, improving their ten talents, and, in old age, recline in the easy chairs of competence and comfort, and in their final exit, may they all obtain seats in that glorious train, whose conductors are the angels of light, and whose depot is the paradise of God.

This sentiment was received with applause.

THE PRESIDENT—I am sorry there is no one here who can rise from his seat in response to this sentiment, brace his back, extend his arm, and give us a "stretcher."

One of the manufacturers alluded to in the sentiment, it was hoped would be present to respond; but as neither of them was present, MR. BROWN, of East Princeton, said:

I find myself, ladies and gentlemen, very much in the position of the schoolmaster of old times. You recollect it was the custom to make considerable preparation for examination, and it was thought best by some, where they had not made much advancement, to let each member of the school know his position, so that he could answer the question given him readily. Well, it so happened, one of the boys was taken sick, and the teacher did not recollect that, and put the questions in their order, one of which related to the Catholic Church. When that question was put, there was no response; but finally a boy spoke up and said: "The boy who believes in the Catholic Church, is at home, sick abed." So it appears there is no response here, because the gentleman who was expected to do it is absent.

Mr. Mirick, of East Princeton, read a rhymed response from J. W. NYE, who was not able to be present.

> When God in Eden's pleasant bowers
> Placed the first happy, human pair,
> I wonder how they passed the hours
> Without a settee or a chair!
>
> Perchance some stone or mound sufficed
> To sit upon while living there ;
> They doubtless would have been surprised
> If they had seen a Princeton chair.

10

Now men, alas, have learned to cheat,
　And little for each other care ;
And manufacturers compete
　In turning out the *cheapest* chair.

Within our humble vale we'll strive
　To busy be, and banish care,
We also calculate to drive
　Up nothing but a *first rate* chair.

Thanks for the sentiment so kind,—
　So full of wishes good and rare,
And may its author ever find,
　When he sits down, an *easy* chair.

No. 7. *The Natural Scenery of Princeton*—While her hills and valleys spread out for the eye of man a rich and bounteous feast, *Old Wachusett*, robed in beauty and grandeur, sits Queen of the scene, and with her waving forest beckons all true lovers of nature to the banquet.

The President called upon THOMAS H. RUSSELL, ESQ., of Boston, to respond.

It is no easy matter, Mr. President, to respond, in suitable terms, to this remembrance of the chief distinction in our natural scenery. It would doubtless be best done in the fewest words. Nothing better can be said, than, *there it stands—it speaks for itself*. Whether I say so or not, *there* it *does* stand, and *does* speak for itself. It were safe to attempt a word in behalf of our "Old Wachusett," behind its back, or in its absence.

I have had the opportunity of seeing something of the mountain scenery of New England and its vicinity ; and while the Holyoke, the Catskill, the Kearsage, the Monadnock, the Green, the Red, and the White, have, each and all, varying characteristics of beauty and grandeur, none surpass our own Wachusett in its most marked and noticeable features of beauty and loveliness. A well defined, isolated, symmetrical cone, rising far above all immediate surroundings, it opens to the view a complete and unbroken circle. In the midst of a country fully and completely subdued to the uses of civilized life, it presents, in no view, anything of the wild or solitary; covered with a primeval growth of forest from base to summit, it reveals nothing rugged, and, in the symmetrical outline of its ascent, loses even the true measure of its massive proportions. It has not, in this hilly country, the more extensive water views of some of its rivals; but few can lay claim to so exclusive a local pre-eminence. As one stands on its well defined summit, the eye rests on no view-obstructing neighbor; the heavens spring from an horizon, a seeming true level, and arch above in a perfect hemisphere; the distant surface of the earth from the same horizon, seeming at the observer's own level, (I know not by what visual law,) sweeps down in a perfect concave to the mountain in its center. As one turns on this center of a seeming grand concave, the eye travels a complete panoramic circle of loveliness; an unbroken range of town and village, lawn, field, and forest, with silver tracery of streams; and, here and there dotting the surface, now expanding, and now hiding in some woody recess, many sweet lakes, in their placid waters mirroring all surrounding beauty; while everywhere are seen evident marks of the human industry, that has subdued and rules over all.

Standing on some of our New England mountains, and looking upon a vast surrounding of mountain upon mountain, and wild unbroken forest, without sign of man, the mind is oppressed with the solitary grandeur and sublimity of the scene, and the awfulness of the presence; but on the Wachusett, you feel that grandeur is refined of all that is fearful, and one seems to repose as on the ancient watch-tower of the vineyard, in the very midst of a scene of peace, life, and loveliness.

Mr. President, those of us to whom the natural scenery we look upon to-day is the first we saw of all the great and beautiful works of God, may well love these hills and valleys. We may be pardoned if we dispute the right of distant or other lands or scenes, to diminish ought of that affection and regard.

It is needless to make a weary pilgrimage to the desolate banks of the Nile,—to seek a crumbling pyramid, buried sphinx, or enigmatical hieroglyphic of perished nations,—to delve in the sands of Euphrates' bank, or to climb to the storyless ruins of Baelbec,—it is needless to do all, or any of these things, to stand in the presence of the venerable past, and look on the face of the ancient.

Would you look on *the venerable—the ancient?* Look about you. Have you never thought that, before the history of our race began,—before Moses gave the decalogue to the descendants of Abraham,—before Persian or Greek, Rome or Carthage strove for the mastery of the world, this old sentinel commenced its long watch over these hills and valleys? May not the waters of a general flood have rolled and surged over its top? Have not the storms of six thousand winters beat upon it, and six thousand summers fanned it with their sweet breath? What if no human eye rested on it for long ages, and these lovely habitations, the great architect prepared for man, waited long their coming tenants, even their savage precursors of civilized life? "A thousand years are as one day," and "one day as a thousand years" with him, in whose mysterious Providence

"Full many a gem of purest ray serene,
    The dark, unfathomed caves of ocean bear ;
Full many a flower is born to blush unseen,
    And waste its sweetness on the desert air."

How shortly after the discovery of this Continent, this eminence became known, is not certain. Certain it is, that Governor Winthrop, as early as 1631, January 27, and some company with him, ascended Charles river, eight miles beyond Watertown, and there, on the west side of a hill, on a very high rock, they "might see all over Neipnett, and a very high hill due west, about forty miles off."

This was our Wachusett two hundred and twenty-eight years ago,—away back almost to the days of good Queen

Bess,—eleven years after the landing of Plymouth, and almost the time of the settlement of Boston. How much of the world's history has transpired since Governor Winthrop, on that Wednesday, more than two centuries ago, looked on yonder, to us, familiar mountain,—a period almost spanning the civilized history of the Western Continent. It has witnessed the birth and vigorous growth of the western nations, as it had before witnessed the all unwritten history of that strange people who possessed the land before us, and yet seems to-day no older.

Sir, the great duties of life, are not those to which the heart most willingly turns. It marks the beneficence of the Author of the Universe, that above this fundamental permanency of nature, there rests a mantle of change. The phenominal world is all change. The day has a morning, noon, night; the year a Spring, a Summer, a Winter. Life has an infancy of weakness, a manhood of strength, an age of decay and death. If all about us were permanent,—no falling leaf—no darkening evening—no decay or death of beauty—no alarm to break our repose,— man would be in danger of forgetting the great purpose of his being, and in fancied fruition of a fleeting present, fail to lay hold of the permanent and eternal.

It is the benevolence of God that, while we gather here to-day, is mantling thus our hoary monitor in his garments of bright, but swift passing beauty,—benevolence, that awakens a new life with an opening Spring, clothes a world in beauty, and swift turns that beauty to ashes.

> " Where are the flowers, the fair young flowers,
>   That lately sprang and stood
> In brighter light and softer airs,
>   A beauteous sisterhood ?
> Alas ! they all are in their graves ;
>   The gentle race of flowers
> Are lying in their lowly beds,
>   With the fair and good of ours."

How largely we ourselves participate in this element of change. On these hills we have played away our youth—

we cannot come back and play away our age. Our companions are gone,—the sports of youth have no longer keenness and relish. We looked then on children, and now, coming back, can hardly believe they are men. The fresh bloom we used to see and look for—ah! it belongs now to other and new faces. We knock at this door and that, but no familiar form responds. Alas! the places that once knew them know them no more—and so *one hundred years*.

The fathers—where are they? The children—their children's children—where are they? Three generations have now lived under the shadow of this goodly mountain; have looked on its familiar face; have struggled with life and its duties, as we do now; have cherished its hopes, its affections, and borne its griefs, disappointments and sorrows; have tilled these fair lands, and peacefully rest in the bosom of mother earth.

Life is a warfare that knows no rest. The order is always, *march!* We are of the grand procession of our country. The youngest of us begin to feel the pressure, and hear the admonitory steps of those who come after us. Happy, indeed, if, as we pass along this day under the shadow of our native Wachusett, we seize the great lesson of the moment. Mark the swinging pendulum of Summer and Winter, sunshine and shadow, that measures off the days of the year, as of our fathers. They sleep—*ours* to-day the battle of life. If I may be permitted with a text to put an end to a discourse, perhaps too largely tinged with the hues of surrounding nature to indicate the thought I would bear away from these pleasant festivities—from these sacred memories—as our fresh purpose, as we lead the van a second coming century, I would say: " Whatsoever things are *true*, whatsoever things are *honest*, whatsoever things are *just*, whatsoever things are *pure*, whatsoever things are *lovely*, whatsoever things are *of good report*, if there be any virtue, and if there be any praise, think on *these* things."

No. 8. *The Young Ladies of Princeton*—May their virtues be larger than their skirts, and their faults smaller even than their bonnets.

(Laughter.)

No. 9. *The Mothers of Princeton*—As patterns of virtuous industry, of mental and moral worth, may they be reproduced in each succeeding generation.

No. 10. To-day, while we thank God that our cup of blessings is *so* full, let us also pray, that each succeeding generation may possess a Fuller.

Response by Rev. ARTHUR B. FULLER, of Watertown.

Mr. President, and Ladies and Gentlemen:—It seems to me that history is ever repeating itself, and as though we had, to-day, one instance of which Solomon tells us is a truth, that "there is nothing new under the sun." It is not the first time that a Rev. Mr. Fuller has addressed the inhabitants of Princeton, although *this* Mr. Fuller has never had the pleasure of seeing them face to face before, or of grasping their hands, and telling them that those who bear the name and cherish the memory of their first minister, cherish, also, a love for this place and this people.

I have been very much gratified, Mr. President, in coming here, and gratified with what I have heard and what I have seen. I might pass some few criticisms on this place, if I chose. I might go back to Boston, and say that everybody who came here "got high." I had to—I think every one does who succeeds in reaching this elevated place. I might, too, go to State street, or Wall street, and tell our merchants, if they want to "raise the wind," they had better come here. (Laughter.)

I was a little fearful for the practical result of my poetical friend's address. He talked about squeezing *hands*; but I found I got squeezed all over in passing through the crowded aisles of your church, this morning. Truly, there I found a warm welcome, even on this cold and windy day.

I believe a part of my grandfather's ministry here was a stormy one, and I was gratified when I received a note from your Committee, inviting me here to say a few words in reference to him.

I was glad to hear my friend, *Major* Cobb, " shell out," so abundantly, the *kernels*, out of which good intellectual bread could be made. Yes, it has been pleasant to see my classmates here to-day,—the friend who preceded me,(T. H. Russell, Esq.,) and my friend Cobb,—and that our good class of 1843 was thus represented here by us three—a trinity that I can believe in—three in one—three persons, but one in purpose, mind and spirit. But I did not come up here to speak in this strain. As I was thinking of coming, I was asked by your Orator, for some ancient documents which were in my possession. I was astonished, on searching an old trunk in my attic, to see how many venerable papers, pertaining to your history, I had inherited. . I have in my hand the first Covenant* of this church, with the names of the original settlers on it. Here is the name of Robert Keyes, whose lost daughter has been so touchingly alluded to, in the Oration and Poem of to-day. Here, too, are the names of Mirick, and Mosman, and Hastings, and many another of your early settlers, written in their own hands.

Here is the first Thanksgiving Sermon ever preached in this place. I have, too, an ancient deed—a certified copy —by which Wachusett mountain was given to my grandfather, and I have come to look after my property a little, to know whether it has been entered upon, and whether my timber has been, any of it, removed, without my consent. I fear, alas, that some subsequent deed, however, makes that beautiful mountain the property of some other than me.

I have, also, here, a letter from Governor Gill, presenting the first Bible ever publicly read in this town ; and, also, mentioning to my grandfather a very beautiful lady, who

*This document, with that recording the marriages and deaths of the first settlers, was presented, by Mr. Fuller, to the first church, through Rev. Mr. Briggs, at the close of the Centennial Celebration.

resided out of Princeton, I am sorry to say, and whom Mr. Gill believed would have made my grandfather a most excellent wife.

Here, too, is a newspaper, which was conned diligently, and contains an account of the Massacre in Boston, March 5th, 1770. This is the *only* copy that came into this town. It was gazed at by eager eyes, till hearts throbbed and tears wet the page. It told of slaughter, and an event which made the heart beat high, and the very turf throb beneath their feet; and ultimately, doubtless, influenced them to go where they could, as soldiers, avenge that and other later atrocious crimes against liberty.

But I wish to establish definitely the fact, that my grandfather was a true patriot in those " times which tried men's souls," and in favor of the great principles of the Declaration of Independence. As a specimen of some of the arguments used to create a contrary impression at the time, I will state one. A man got up in town meeting here, in 1775, and said: " I know Mr. Fuller is not pious, and is a Tory, for I caught hold of him suddenly, the other evening, and in his surprise, he said: 'Let alone of me, by George!' Now as he said ' by,' he could not be pious; and he must have meant George the Third, and of course, then, if he would swear by *him*, he must be a Tory." Such, sir, were the ridiculous arguments, which were deemed sufficient, in the excited, almost frantic period of which I am speaking, when a righteous jealousy for freedom, assuredly led to some unjust suspicions of those no less friendly to liberty than the most zealous patriots of Princeton.

But, on this subject, I propose not simply to make corrections, but to give *proof*, and that of an undeniable character—proof in the handwriting of my grandfather, giving his public declaration of his opinions, read in open town meeting, in 1775. These papers were not put upon record then, though referred to in the town records. It was suffered to be lost, but, fortunately, I have the

11

original document in my hand, here and now. It explains every circumstance which made Rev. Timothy Fuller suspected then, and clearly declares his agreement with the principles of the Revolution, and his readiness, even, to fight in their behalf.

I have come to vindicate his memory; and it is as important for you to know, that you never had a minister who was not true to liberty, as it is for me to be able to say that I had no such ancestor. Let me, then, read from these ancient documents, the originals of which were once read in Princeton, in 1775.

" *To the Committee of Correspondence, Mr. Thomson, Chairman, to be laid before the Town :—*

GENTLEMEN :

I am very much surprised to find that any among you should suspect me of entertaining Principles inconsistent with ye cause of liberty, since I have uniformly espoused and supported it, both in public and private, from ye very beginning of our controversy with Great Britain.

I have always submitted to ye advice of Congresses, both provincial and continental ; subscribed with my Hand ye Non Importation and Non Consumption agreement ; strictly adhered to it; have never opposed any public Measure taken to preserve ye Rights and Privileges of ye People ; and though I have thought that ye people have run into some Irregularities, yet not more than might be expected from every opposition to unconstitutional and oppressive acts of Government. It has always been my firm Opinion, that ye Parliament of Great Britain, in exercising ye Right claimed of binding America in all cases whatsoever, would reduce us to absolute Slavery. I have, years ago, laid aside ye use of Tea, and urged you to do ye same, that we might defeat their Design of raising a Revenue from us, encouraged our manufactures, and pressed a Union in this and all ye Colonies, that our Resistance might be formidable and successful. *   *   *   *   *   *   *

I think we have Reason and a Right to Complain, and when our Complaints are not heard, and our Grievances redressed, we have a Right to resist. We of Right ought to be as free as ye People of England, according to Charter.   *   *   *   *   *   *   *

I am sorry to be so unhappy as to fall under the suspicion of being unfriendly to ye Common cause. I believe I am as hearty a Lover of my Country, as any among you, or any in ye Country. I am ready, when Necessary, to fight in ye Defense of it, and of Religion. I think ministers are not called to War, unless ye rest of ye Community are unable to defend it without them, and in such a case I am ready to do my part ; I would not count my Life dear to me, but would brave every Danger of War." * * * * * * * *

In conclusion : " What your design is in calling me in Question, I may not determine. If any were so mistaken and ignorant of my Principles, as to be really jealous, I am sorry ; but I am willing to give account of myself, without being offended, and am persuaded that what I have offered above will give you entire Satisfaction as to my firm attachment to ye Principles of civil liberty, and to remove every doubt from your minds ; if not, I am willing to carry ye matter before the provisional or continental Congress.

TIMOTHY FULLER.

PRINCETON, May 29, 1779."

This was read, June 2d, 1775, to the town. Another paper was sent to the same Committee, to be laid before the town, June 7th, of which I give the most important part.

" To the Committee, William Thomson, Chairman, to be laid before the Town :—

GENTLEMEN :

I beg Leave now, to make some Additions with respect to several things in the Paper which I read to ye Town, on Friday last. I do not believe ye Parliament of Great Britain hath any Right to make any Law whatever binding on ye Colonies, nor to lay any Taxes or duties on us, without our Consent. I am clearly of opinion, that ye acts, called ye Boston Port Bill, that for Altering the Government of this Province, and that for sending Criminals to Great Britain for Tryal, and ye Quebec bill, are unreasonable and unjust, and what ye Parliament have no right to enact, and that ye Colonies are so far from being obliged to submit to them, that it would be criminal in them, and they would be ruined by such submission. It is our Duty, at present, to unitedly exert ourselves to ye utmost, with Dependence on the blessing of Heaven on our righteous Cause, to resist, by Force and Arms, the Execution of those Acts. I look upon it (as) a favorable Providence, that the Colonies of this Continent, and this in particular, are generally so happily agreed in asserting and defending our civil and religious Rights, against ye Invasions of the British Ministry and Parliament, and their venal Army. It is, I think, ye Duty of every man to encourage, and according to his Ability, to promote ye Success of ye Army, now raised by this Colony, for its necessary Safety and Defense."

I think a man who is ready, if necessary, to fight for the cause, or who offers himself as a Chaplain in her army, would be acknowledged as a true patriot. And it is gratifying to know, that the people of Princeton came to the same conclusion in after years, that he dwelt here among you, and was chosen your Representative to the Convention, Governor Gill being the rival candidate. Nor can I feel other than an honorable pride, in saying, that his descendants have uniformly loved liberty. It was a granddaughter of your first minister, who sought to staunch the wounds of those who were fighting in the cause of liberty in a foreign land, who remained in the city of Rome, during its eventful seige, in 1848, and did all a brave and noble woman could do for the cause of liberty. Such noble fruit could have grown on no unworthy tree of ancestors ; and I rejoice to say, as a matter of simple truth and justice, that the principles of freedom, cherished by my ancestors, have been, and are cherished by all his descendants, and that to-day, however on other points they may differ, there is not one who does not long for the diffusion of civil and religious liberty, in our own and all lands, till at last your sun shall not rise on a tyrant or master, or rest on any who are oppressed or enslaved.

No. 11. *Bachelors*—Left alone, as they *wish*, will have no history in the next celebration.

There was no response.

No. 12. *The Medical Profession*—The ignorance of mankind with reference to the laws of life and health, creates its necessity. In the good time coming, their prescriptions will be preventatives of, rather than cures for, disease, Till then, may their pills and powders be harmless.

To this sentiment, Dr. NATHAN ALLEN, of Lowell, responded. He said :

I wish to speak a few words, as the only representative of my profession present ; and I wish to speak in behalf of the town, in reference to medicine and health. We had, in the address this forenoon, an account of a physician who occupied the chair in town meetings, and held many high offices. For the last hundred years, we have had a noble order of men, well educated in the medical profession, here.

I believe there has been no irregular practitioners in this town, and it has been remarkable for being a healthful place.

I wish to state three facts. The first is, that, according to the statistics, there has not been a town in this County, that could compare with this in respect to healthfulness. The rate of mortality is less than in any other town, being only one in ninety-three, for many years. But in Sterling, it is one in sixty-seven; in Holden, one in fifty-six; in Westminster, one in seventy-five; in Worcester, one in forty-eight; while in Boston, it is one in thirty-eight. I find on turning to the record of deaths, last year, that seventeen persons died, of whom eight were over seventy years of age, and three were between eighty-five and ninety.

Another fact is, that the average length of life here, has been remarkable. This we can show by the ages of persons who have died in a long series of years. The average age here has been over fifty years, while in all the other towns of the County, it has been less. In Worcester, it has been but twenty-two years, so that persons may expect to live twice as long here as in Worcester. There have been but two epidemics here in many years.

Another fact, which is creditable to this town, is that a large donation was given, many years ago, by one of the citizens of this town, Dr. Ward Nicholas Boylston, for the benefit of the medical profession of this State. That donation was given in such a way that large sums are distributed annually, for the encouragement of students of the medical profession. That sum, put to interest at the time it was given, would now amount to more than seventy thousand dollars.

We see why it is that people will come here from abroad; and they will come more and more, where such fresh air, and such wholesome diet may be obtained. People who live here do not realize, nor have any adequate idea of their privileges.

Only five or six persons from this town, have entered the medical profession. When I have looked at the history of this town, and considered its advantages with reference to health, I felt proud to refer to it.

I will merely add a sentiment:

The Inhabitants of Princeton, and the Medical Profession—May their relations in the next hundred years, show as much consistency and liberality as they have in the past hundred years.

No. 13. *The next Centennial Anniversary*—May our children have reason to venerate us, as we to-day do our fathers.

No. 14. *Princeton's Sons*—May their *aim* be as high, their *view* as broad, and their *principles* as *firm* and *deep-rooted*, as their own *Wachusett*.

To this sentiment, JOHN A. DANA, Esq., of Worcester, responded as follows:

Mr. President, Ladies and Gentlemen:—I congratulate you upon the success of this Celebration. Most heartily do I thank you and the people of this my native town, for this opportunity to exchange with each other kindly greetings and joyful congratulations. Pausing here for a little, at the close of the first century of our town's history, recalling pleasant reminiscences of the past, and with mutual good wishes for the future, we will gather new strength to go forth to its duties, with a stronger heart, and a fuller confidence.

Sir, I will yield to no one, in the strong attachment I feel for the place of my birth, the home of my boyhood, the scene of my early joys, and my boyish griefs. My feelings to-day are keenly alive to the sentiment of Goldsmith's lines:

> " Where'er I roam, whatever realms to see,
> My heart, untravel'd, fondly turns to thee.
> * * * * * * * *
> Such is the patriot's boast, where'er we roam,
> His first, best country, ever is at home.
> * * * * * * * *
> Thus every good his native wilds impart
> Imprints the patriot passion on his heart;
> And e'en those ills that round his mansion rise,
> Enhance the bliss his scanty fund supplies;
> Dear is that shed to which his soul conforms,

And dear that hill which lifts him to the storms ;
And as a child, when scaring sounds molest,
Clings close and closer to the mother's breast—
So the loud torrent and the whirlwind's roar,
But bind him to his native mountains more.''

The sentiment to which you do me the honor to invite me
to respond, brings me back to my home, by the reference
you have made to that mountain, to which I have so often
looked when away, and to which I have, with a glow of
pride, pointed many as my native mountain. Why, sir, the
time has been, when I thought it the highest mountain in
the world ! However much wiser I may be to-day in this
respect, I have never seen, nor do I ever expect to see,
any mountain whose view will stir in my heart more
pleasant emotions, than are always excited when I look
upon its familiar face. It is an honest old mountain, and
if it is not quite so high as some, I am sure it is as old as
any, and will last as long. But, sir, the sentiment looks to
something else ; it looks to the end and object of all our
lives, and the means by which we may make them a success.
As a life without purpose can never be useful, so, without
a broad view, and a firm foundation on fixed principles
of action, it can never be successful.

The young are often told to set their aims high. Often
have I heard it in that little red school-house, and this was
told us in such a way, that we were led to think that the
wise course was to fix the mind upon some particular
object, some place of honor or trust, some high position
of power or influence,—that we should single out some one
of these, as a particular object of pursuit, to attain which,
all our energies should be directed.

I do not intend to usurp the prerogative of the pulpit,
and read you a sermon on this occasion, though it is much
easier to preach than to practice. But I will suggest
whether we should not labor to inculcate in others, and
whether each should not bring himself to feel that all the
objects of life, worthy of pursuit by a rational being, should
be pursued as a *means* to an end, and not the end itself,

and that end a two-fold one,—self-culture and development in the individual, and usefulness to mankind.

Now we all know, that but few can attain to places of eminence, as commonly received and understood. How few of the many who start in the race for wealth, power or station, attain the position for which they strive. They all start with high hopes, with a high, it may be with a noble, ambition. The motto with them is, "*aut Cæsar, aut nullus,*" and they usually verify the motto—but their verification is very unfortunate.

What I would urge is, that each should endeavor to develop in himself a complete manhood; that each should inculcate all the faculties of his nature,—physical, mental and moral,—by such pursuits as are best fitted to his particular organization, without regard to any particular end to be attained, but the general one I have named, and we shall find we have each a position of greatness, which will well reward all our labor. By such a course as this, we shall all find enough to do at home; we shall all have a business for life on our hands. We need not go far in search of labor or duty; it lies all around us, and the future, about which we have so much solicitude, will become *the present*, for the surest way to know our duty in the future, is to do the duty that lies next us.

And we shall also find, that true greatness lies not in any particular station in life, but in every station. It needs not wealth or rank to give it power; it has a power all its own. It shines as well in the cottage of the poor, as in the mansion of the rich.

> " What tho' on hamely fare we dine,
>   Wear hoddin grey and a' that:
> Gie fools their silk and knaves their wine,
>   A *man's* a man for a' that.
> An honest man tho' e'er sae poor,
>   Is king of men for a' that."

I close with this sentiment:

His aims are high who aims a complete, perfect manhood. His view must be broad, and his principles firm, who will attain it.

No. 15. *Our Festal Day*—We, this day, tie the nuptial knot between the past and coming century. And our Mother,* though hoary with age, is, (we are happy to know,) vigorous and blithe as ever, and many of her sons and daughters are present to grace the ceremony.

It was expected this sentiment would have been responded to by Colonel HOWE, of Rutland; but owing to the lateness of the hour, he was obliged to leave the house, before the sentiment was read.

The following is a volunteer sentiment, left by Colonel HOWE:

The Citizens of Princeton—Their past has been marked by enterprise, benevolence, and prosperity. May their future be distinguished by all those virtues which elevate and adorn the human family.

No. 16. *The Wachusett Cornet Band*—May their lives be so pure, and their strains of music so ennobling, that this old monarch of hills shall proudly own his namesake.

Responded to by the Band.

The meeting then adjourned till seven o'clock in the evening.

EVENING MEETING.

At a little after seven o'clock, the Church was pretty well filled again, agreeably to the adjournment, and the President, having called the meeting to order, said:

Ladies and Gentlemen:—Permit me, once more, in behalf of our vigilant Committee of Arrangements, in behalf of the legal voters of Princeton, by whose act we have this day assembled, to extend to you the right hand

*A large portion of Princeton was, at its incorporation, taken from Rutland.

of fellowship, and to thank you all for the interest you have taken, on this occasion, which interest has brought you together again this evening, to listen to these closing services. It was a custom of our fathers, to look to God in all their town meetings,—to that Being whose mercies are new every morning, and fresh every evening and every moment. Shall we, in imitation of their example, look to Him on this occasion? Will Rev. Mr. Cowles lead us in prayer?

Prayer was then offered by Rev. JOHN P. COWLES, of Ipswich, a former Pastor in Princeton.

After music by the Band, the next regular sentiment was read, as follows:

No. 17. *The Second Centennial Celebration*—The heroic and successful resistance of our ancestors to British tyranny, secured freedom to one race of one age. May it be the glad privilege of those who shall stand here to celebrate one hundred years this day, that the *nobler* patriotism, and *holier self-sacrifice* of the friends of unrestricted human rights in this country, have bequeathed impartial liberty to *every tribe of every race*, forevermore.

Mr. E. H. HEYWOOD, of Worcester, called upon to respond, said:

It may seem unfortunate that it should fall to me " to give the improvement," as the old Puritans would say, of the sentiment just read, fellowshipped as I am with a class of persons who have the reputation of not being very economical of truth, who sometimes have a weakness for telling the whole truth, in dealing with the question of freedom. I appreciate the feelings of that slip of the clerical profession, who, caught holding forth in strait Puritan Boston, without proper authority, was called to order by one who sat in Moses' seat. "But don't the Bible say, we must preach the Gospel to every critter?" asked the sprig. "Yes," replied the venerable divine; "but it don't say that every critter must preach the Gospel."

I find that, as early as 1763, the settlers of this town passed resolutions, showing a clear-sighted, resolute and unswerving devotion to the principles of that inspired and immortal declaration, which, in 1776, leaped from the brain of Jefferson, full-armed for the revolutionary conflict. Subsequently, they dismissed their minister, (Rev. Mr. Fuller,) for entertaining, as they erroneously supposed, Tory proclivities—then inaugurating the itinerant method, so popular here, for Princeton has always settled its ministers on horseback. Thus early did our fathers evince a faith in principle, and a spirit of self-sacrifice of every worldly interest, in adherence to the cause of freedom. They saw that human rights are antecedent to all human governments, and hence above the reach or refusal of all human laws. They made institutions for man. The political and ecclesiastical policy of the present day, makes man for institutions. It circumscribes the boundaries of human rights; spells negro with two *gs*; preaches Jesus and practices Judas. Our ancestors overleaped the fences of custom and tradition—were the "rebels," the "insurrectionists," and "madmen" of their day. Hence, their lesson to us is: "Break with the huckstering 'law and order' of your age; project your thoughts from behind institutions; build on ideas; trample under foot all compromising organizations; 'be governed by the laws of God, until you can make better.'"

Some years later, Mr. Fuller returning—a prophet to be honored in his own country—showed, conclusively, that he was right on the question of freedom. In the State Convention, to ratify the Federal Constitution, he voted *against* that iniquitous instrument, on the ground of its pro-slavery clauses. I am proud that the representative of my native town took so noble a position in that crisis, so fatal to the black man,—proud that the first clergyman of this district, bore so high a moral testimony to the politicians of his age. The test of principle is to disagree with our immediate cotemporaries, when conscience bids. Mr.

Fuller, doing that, proved his superiority. He was taller than his peers—a moral Wachusett, crowned by the light of opposite centuries. Let us thank God that this heroic minister of Christ, had the moral courage to outface his compromising fellows and repudiate a constitution that consigned the black man to perpetual slavery.

I do not wish to preach you an anti-slavery lecture, but I must say, I was saddened this morning, on looking around, to find not a single motto—significant of the fact, that four million slaves are crushed under the political and ecclesiastical institutions of this country—not one word to alleviate the ineffable woes that weigh upon their hearts. Are not the sainted insurrectionists of '76 still on the side of the oppressed? Do not they yearn to-day, from their higher seats, towards these millions of " suffering and dumb " victims of a bondage, " one hour of which," Jefferson being the judge, " is fraught with more misery than whole ages of that which we rose in rebellion to oppose ?"

Pluck aside the centuries, and see how far we have strayed from that sublime ancestry, which " began with Puritanism and the wilderness ; " from that martyr faith, which, hurling British tyranny across the Atlantic, sounded boldly out into the great deep of equal rights, the Columbus of a true popular sovereignty. In 1641, Massachusetts, young, weak, destitute as an orphan girl, spread her arms "to all who could fly to her from the tyranny and oppression of their persecutors," and pledged them protection and maintenance at the public cost. In 1859, rich, luxurious, powerful, studded all over with churches, colleges, and temples of justice, the Legislature refusing to shelter the hounded fugitive from oppression, deliberately votes, (the representative of this town concurring,*) that our soil, hallowed with heroes' graves, shall continue open ground for the slave-hunter ! Thank God for Massachutetts ! She was the first of civilized States in history, to abolish slavery by law. It was done in 1780, and the glorious event should be distinguished by a red letter day in our Calender. But in 1789, she went into partnership with slave dealers, and tho firm is yet undissolved. When Webster was kicking in his cradle, Washington wrote to New Hampshire for the return of a fugitive woman. But, said he, if the moral sentiment of the people is against it, let her go. In 1859, Massachusetts erects a statue to the man, who, beyond all others, has insulted tho moral sentiment of New England, by commanding her to "conquer her prejudices" in favor of liberty, and return men to bondage, "with alacrity." But why travel so far from home? I have told you how the early settlers of this town, rude, untaught, scarcely able to wring a subsistence from these unthankful hills, risked the ruin of their church, and the loss of educational advantages, by hurrying from their sacred desk, a minister, on mere suspicion of indifference to the interests of freedom, and of sympathizing with a comparatively respectable despotism beyond the Atlantic. I would gladly forget to say, did truth and the solemn monitions of this hour allow it, that lately there stood in this pulpit, with the consent of these pews, the great New England apologist of the most cruel and remorseless system of bondage in modern history.*

We meet to celebrate the deeds of revolutionists, of traitors, of insurrectionists. To-day, with a chastened, reverent enthusiasm, we take into our hands the consecrated sword, or musket, with which they slew oppressors. We wear next our very hearts, every brave word, whereby they pledged themselves to sink the government, the church, and the world, rather than relinquish justice or liberty. We glory in that congregationalism which made every man a church; in that democracy which made every man a monarchy. Those sainted farmers, play-fellows of these venerable hills, wherever they walked, society heaved with the volcanic throes of revolt. We are all the

* See Note.

children, the heirs apparent, of treason and rebellion. Put your ear to the ground, and you will hear the echoing, earthquake tread of the impending second American Revolution. This very week, its Bunker's Hill was fought at Harper's Ferry. The timid, faithless toryism of to-day, pales and trembles at the crack of insurgent rifles, whose echoes still linger among the Alleghanies and Shenandoahs. John Brown, braver than Warren, more self-sacrificing than Lafayette, with his Spartan score of followers, throws himself against a gigantic despotism, in defence of the principles of the fathers. From these sacred graves, on which we stretch ourselves to-day, they speak: "Go thou and do likewise; be true to our memory; execute justice for the oppressed; launch upon equal inalienable rights, and let God take care of the consequences."

As Luther said, "God never can do without brave men." The age of brute force, the reign of bullets, is over. Ideas are gradually ascending to absolute power. It is our privilege to rely upon moral force agitation—upon the omnipotence of abstract principles. The times "demand an arm of tougher sinew than the sword." It is for us to side with the oppressed and down-trodden in the great *moral* Bunker Hills and Solferinos of human conflict, to make ourselves of no reputation, and suffer the loss of all things, if need be, in defence of Jesus in the "little ones." Every crown of glory must first be a crown of thorns. As for me, I believe in the inalienable and absolute right of every man to "life, liberty, and the pursuit of happiness." I am for the immediate and unconditional emancipation of every slave of every race, clime, or condition. In the great conflict for the rights of black men, now shaking this country to its foundations, "no union with slaveholders," is the highest moral ground, the only Christian position, the only Pisgah that overlooks the promised land of impartial liberty from this wilderness of compromise. Our fathers rest from their labors. The beloved sleep well. We, also, are before the world, who will judge us according to our works. To equal our predecessors, we must surpass them. To do as much, we must do more.

" New occasions teach new duties ; Time makes ancient good uncouth ;
They must upward still, and onward, who would keep abreast of Truth.
Lo, before us gleam her campfires ! We ourselves must Pilgrims be ;
Launch our Mayflower, and steer boldly through the desperate winter sea,
Nor attempt the Future's portal with the Past's blood-rusted key."

*NOTE.—The undersigned, a majority of the Committee, having this report in charge, (the minority disclaiming it their province to judge, or express an opinion in the matter,) deem it but simple justice to state, that in their judgement, the remarks of Mr. Heywood, in the particulars indicated by reference to this note, were untrue in point of fact; and, moreover, were an unwarranted, though we charitably believe, an unintentional trespass upon the proprieties of the occasion.

CHARLES RUSSELL,
WILLIAM B. GOODNOW,
EDWARD E. HARTWELL.

Rev. Dr. ALLEN was again invited to speak. He said :

It has been mentioned to-day, and has been often mentioned, as a thing very peculiar in the history of Princeton, that a people so intelligent, considerate and conservative as they have always been, should have such a history with regard to the ministry in the town. Since I came into the town, a man said to me, that the present minister of the Church here, is the twelfth or thirteenth, in succession, and that no man has ever died here, holding the pastoral office. He said, further, that the town did not contain the remains of a single minister of the Gospel, of any denomination. I, however, satisfied him of the fact, that the old burying ground, on the hill, does contain the remains of a native of this town, who was a minister of the Gospel.

Why is it, that among people so considerate, and so conservative, no minister has ever retained the pastoral office till called away by death ? I put this question to myself, and I answer it by saying, that it is because the people have been so religous, and had such exact and clear views of divine truth. I will mention, as an illustration, an anecdote. A gentleman was invited to become a pastor of one of the Churches here. After considering the invitation for sometime, he declined. He did not, then, give any reason; but as the people expressed some disappointment at his not accepting their invitation, he told them that he did not decline the invitation for want of salary, for they had offered him as much as he expected. To some of my friends in another town, he gave the following reason: "When I learned how well informed the people were on all the doctrines of Christianity, and when I saw every eye fixed on me, and scanning me, I felt as if I was preaching to an assembly of Puritan divines, and that I was not competent to become the minister of such a people. I declined the invitation solely on that ground." That minister is still living. I think the strong religious character, the clear and exact views of divine truth, and the great importance which the people here attached to *every part* of the system of religion which they had embraced, has had much to do with the changes in their ministry.

I have heard people in the towns around say: "How the people in Princeton quarrel about religion." But it was no quarrelling, in their view. They were only "contending earnestly for the faith once delivered to the Saints." They could not only tell what they believed, but give reason upon reason, from morning till night. It was no mere disputation, no quarrelling, no wrangling. No. They did it from the highest and holiest feelings.

I will make a remark upon one thing, which I believe is not alluded to in the histories of this town. There are some things concerning individuals, and families, and communities, which can be learned only by observation. It was remarked that the people of this town were a noble people in their intellectual character, and in their political and religious principles and conduct. But they were a noble class of people in another respect—physically, bodily. I never saw such a generation of men. I have had much observation of mankind, and a large experience of the world, but I never saw such men as were here forty and fifty years ago. I presume those who are old, and growing old, like myself, will be of the same opinion. A stranger in the town, once attended the old church on the hill, and he afterward remarked how he was struck with the appearance of the people. He never saw such people, men and. women, sons and daughters. He said he was reminded of the story in the book of Joshua, where the spies reported that they saw the Anakims—giants—in the land, and "we were in our own sight as grasshoppers, and so were we in their sight." I remembered, said he, that the Bible says the Anakims lived "in the hill country," and I supposed they were extinct, till I came here; but I find they are still living "in the hill country," around about Wachusett, and among the other hills of Princeton.

The next sentiment was :

No. 18. *Old Princeton*—The good old days of Princeton, made glorious by the solid worth, true valor, and wise patriotism of our fathers. May her sons perpetuate her virtues.

Mr. EVERETT—The next sentiment has reference to the old men and women who still linger with us, but who will soon pass away to the spirit land.

No. 19. *The Old Men and Women of Princeton*—May their last days be their best, and their last pleasures the sweetest. May their declining sun shed mellow beams of light on their posterity, and set in glory.

THE PRESIDENT—If there is no one prepared to respond to this sentiment, we will proceed to the next.

MR. EVERETT—I wish we might have some volunteer sentiments, with such remarks as gentlemen may please to offer. We have shaken the hearts of many friends through their hands, to-day, and I would like to hear from some of them this evening.

THE PRESIDENT—I am happy to know that Capt. Amos
13

Merriam, from the city of spindles, (Lowell,) is here. We shall be pleased to hear a word from him.

Capt. MERRIAM being thus called out, said:

I am not a literary man, and you must not expect a long speech from me. I have come up here to-day, tó see and hear, and I have been extremely gratified with what I have seen and heard. I have not been in this town for many years—nearly or quite a quarter of a century—and most of the old inhabitants I recognize to-day. At the time I left the place, there was not a family here that I did not know very well, having occupied a position that led me to a general acquaintance with the people of the town. I was, for many years, a Selectman, and an Overseer of the Poor, and was, also, a Surveyor, so that I was led to know the people in all parts of the town.

I rejoice that I have been permitted to meet so many of you whom I once knew, and to listen to the speeches and sentiments that have been uttered. They have brought back to my mind the sterling virtues of this people. The glory and happiness of the people here, does not consist in their numbers, but in their character, and I think I can bear my testimony fully, that the true character of the people has been expressed in the addresses to which I have had the pleasure of listening to-day.

I will not occupy your time any further, but will offer, as a sentiment, a few words:

> This *Centennial Day* to celebrate we meet,
> Our friends to see, and them to greet.
> Before returns another Anniversary day,
> Three generations will have passed away.
> Then to all that's good and great aspire,
> Like yonder mountain, beckoning higher,
> That Princeton's sons and daughters, yet unborn,
> May bless the world that they adorn.

THE PRESIDENT—We have with us an adopted son, who is somewhat advanced in years, as many of the rest of us are, who has spent many years in Princeton. Let me introduce to you THOMAS WILDER, Esq., of Boston.

Mr. President, Ladies and Gentlemen:—I am happy to embrace this opportunity, to speak of one, whose name has not been much mentioned on this occasion. One, who, half a century ago, was known as Master Woods. In 1802, he conveyed me here from Ashburnham, on the seventh of June. We rode on horseback, and he gave me a very interesting account of every family between these places, pointing out the building where Sam Frost killed his father; the place where the girl was lost; the eastern part of Wachusett, where Frost killed Captain Allen, and the tree on which he climbed to watch the funeral obsequies of his victim.

Master Woods was greeted by his appropriate appellation, by old and young, where he was known. This led the boy who had taken passage upon the same animal with him, without a pillion, to inquire into his antecedents. I soon learned one important fact, that he was the first school-master of the town, and being self-taught, understood how to teach others. Being a man of thought, he strove to promote it by questions suited to elicit thought, and propounding problems to be solved by induction, thus giving to minds a stimulus to develop itself, without depending much upon artificial helps; consequently, a goodly number of intellectual inhabitants, of both sexes, came forward, honorable to the town and country. We need look no further than his own family for illustrations. I might speak of numbers, but will particularize but one, his oldest son by his last wife, Leonard, whose germ, under paternal culture, gave hopeful promise, and who, encouraged by the means of education, which at that time the public schools afforded, graduated at Harvard with the highest honors of the College, and whose writings are said to be the most lucid in the English language, and are read in all the enlightened parts of the world from his works, while he filled the chair of Theology, at Andover Seminary. As like causes produce like effects, it may be seen that the inductive principle which wrought so effectually in Dr. Woods the senior, has been not less so in Dr. Woods junior, now President of Bowdoin College, and who ranks among the first literary men of our country.

Master Woods did a great deal of public business, and my youthful mind was led to inquire, why he had not an Esquire commission. Well, Hon. Moses Gill, being a magistrate sufficient for the business of the town, at that early period, the office, if conferred, would have been rather sinecure. Yet, it was prior to the Gerrymander, synonymous with districting the State for political effect, under the administration of Governor Gerry, which all Federalists thought almost unpardonable. And Rev. Mr. Holcom, of Sterling, at a supper, where poetic freedom was lawful, remarked it was the greatest piece of wickedness ever committed since the rebellion of the fallen angels. How much political hire was used to effect the object, I am unable to say, but Esq.'s came forth like locusts for multitude. Rev. Thomas Mason, of Northfield, Representative of the town for many years, was a son of Princeton, brother of the venerable Joseph Mason, now living on the old farm, between eighty and ninety years old, possessed of mental vigor competent to grapple with almost any subject, and who, by industry, economy and prudence, has furnished a rich legacy for the town. The above reverend gentleman, while sitting upon a splendid horse, was asked why he did not ride an humble ass, as did the great preacher when he entered Jerusalem, replied, he was unwilling to ride a jackass, for Gerry had made them all Esq.'s.

But Esq. Gill, afterwards Lieutenant Governor, conferred upon Master Woods, a more honorable than civil title, even the well-earned appellation of Philosopher, and when he had visitors of philosophic minds, he would send for his Philosopher, and thus introduce him. As he was wont to wear a leather apron at home, he was not careful to put it off on those occasions. It served the double purpose of preserving some portions of his dress, and also, as parchment for data, and a substitute for sand, on which John Newton studied Euclid upon the shores of Africa. When his cogitations were interrupted, he would make a mark to indicate his soundings. His apron was covered with figures, signs, or hieroglyphics.

Mr. President, I am aware by what title I have been introduced to this platform; but, sir, the paper emanating from the Council chamber, came to me most unexpectedly, and knowing there were more magistrates in Ware village, in which place I then resided, than the business of the place demanded, I thought the best use I could make of it would be to lock it up for safe keeping, unaccompanied by any law, hoping it might tend to check the exuberance of Esq.'s.

No. 20. *The memory of our Fathers*—By all their deeds of noble daring, by all their toils and sacrifices in planting institutions for our enjoyment, by their manly virtue and holy example. we will cherish their memories forever.

To this sentiment, the Rev. ARTHUR B. FULLER, of Watertown, responded as follows:

Mr. President, and Ladies and Gentlemen:—I should feel some doubt about trespassing again on your attention and time, were it not that the strain of remark which I felt obliged to offer this afternoon, did not embrace one or two thoughts of that more serious and solemn character, which seem to be becoming to this place and this hour; and as a minister of the gospel of Jesus Christ, standing in the town where an ancestor of mine preached the gospel as he believed it, I feel that there are one or two topics upon which I would speak here and now.

My remarks this afternoon, were for the purpose of removing any undeserved imputation which rested on the patriotism of an ancestor of mine. I propose now to respond to the sentiment just offered, and which seems to me be full of nobleness. I recall much that I have learned from a father and uncles of those who early lived here, for my family have ever treasured each leaf on which the dear name of Princeton was written ; and from those records, I gather some knowledge of their fathers and yours. I gather the impressions which were indelibly written on their minds. I recall some of the accounts which they gave when they came here every year to sing again Zion's songs, and I feel that your ancestors and mine were generally pious, noble men, and that their memory deserves to be cherished. I rejoice in this Centennial Celebration, that it was put into the hearts of this people to come up here and keep this joyous day; and it seems to me we ought to have something more of the serious and devout cast given to our thoughts, which the occasion is so well calculated to suggest.

I remember hearing my grandfather spoken of as one who was instant in season and out of season in his visits to the chambers of the sick and dying; I have a record, kept by him, of the bereavements of the families here.* I find a record of children, breathing out their last sigh ; of old men, by whom he offered the prayer which wafted on the wings of faith the spirit upward; of mothers in Israel giving their last counsel to childhood, as they had given the first smile that was the earliest sunlight that fell on the infant heart. I know, then, something of the fathers of those who dwell here to-day. That grandfather of mine was never accused of any dereliction of duty—his moral integrity was as unmovable as yonder mountain, (Wachusett,) and pointed upward directly as does that hill. And even as to the charge that " he did not catechise the children "—I presume the children were willing to excuse him, if it were so—it was said that they had not

---

* Subsequently presented, with the first covenant, to the Church in Princeton, by the speaker.

the shadow of a reason for the charge that was made against him.

As I came here to-day, and saw your decorations, it seemed to me you scarcely needed to "hang your banner on the outer wall," as I saw the whole landscape decked with beauty, as though decorated to honor the God who had created and fashioned these everlasting hills ; when I saw these rich hues of Autumn so gorgeously displayed, I felt there was a banner floating in every breeze, even as though God had garnished the scene for such an occasion as this.

But, Mr. President, I want to enlarge the sentiment ; I believe in a religion that holds in honor every man and woman who loves God, and Jesus his Son, and humanity, for which that Son died. Love to God, to Christ, to man —that is my Christianity. My creed is, that every human being who endeavors to elevate mankind, deserves to be regarded as a brother, or sister, or mother of every true man. (Applause.) And to all such, of every race of every period, and of each sex, I would fain do impartial justice. I wish now to include the *mothers* of this town in your sentiment of commendation. Too often, in doing justice to man, we forget our sister woman ; too often the memory of the fathers is permitted to overshadow that of noble mothers. I wish to speak of one of those mothers in Israel—my noble and sainted grandmother, once an honored resident of this town. Rev. Timothy Fuller, in going to Sandwich, met a young lady who had charms not only of person, but of mind and spirit, a daughter of the patriotic Rev. Abraham Williams, who sent three sons into the revolutionary fight. That mother said, " Go ; serve your country well ; we will take care of ourselves." One of those sons died in a prison ship of Great Britain. Rev. Timothy Fuller married a sister of those brave young men, Miss Sarah Williams, of Sandwich. During that revolutionary struggle, her father resigned his salary, so that his people might not be impoverished. That woman was

worthy of such a sire, and of the mother who bore her;
she instilled heroic and honorable principles in her children, who, if they did not include my father and uncles, I
should say were an honor to this place. One, my venerable father, became a member of Congress, a Speaker of the
House of Representatives of Massachusetts, a man, of
whom I may, without impropriety, say, that he honored
the place from which he came. (Applause.)

Ah, sir, we are not to forget such mothers, who, in the
quietude of their homes, by the simplicity and beauty of
their daily lives, by their unwearied and unceasing care,
and in answer to their saintly prayers, shape and mould
the hearts and minds of the men of this and all other lands,
and impart to them the larger portion of what in them is
great and noble.

> "The mothers of our forest-land—
>   Their bosoms pillow'd *men*,
> And proud were they by such to stand,
>   In hammock, fort or glen ;
> To load the sure old rifle,
>   To run the leaden ball,
> To watch a battling husband's place,
>   And fill it should he fall ;
> No braver dames had Sparta,
>   No nobler matrons Rome,
> Yet who or lauds or honors them,
>   E'en in their mountain home."

One, at least, Mr. President, shall stand here to-day, and
do them honor, and I know that my word on this topic
will awaken a response in all your hearts.

That " honorable woman " of whom I have spoken, and
who once dwelt amid these beautiful scenes, and loved and
cherished her country's cause, and was willing, as was
her mother, to sacrifice for it, and even consented that
her worthy husband, your minister, should fight in its
behalf, if need be, (as he bravely proffered this town to
do,) shoulder to shoulder with its patriotic " minute men"—
that woman, I say, was fit to be commemorated to-day as

the ancestor of another woman no less noble, and of whom America is justly proud,—Margaret Fuller,—who was her descendant, who sacrificed so much for liberty in fair Italy, who suffered privation in Rome during its besiegement, and soothed and comforted the wounded Romans, bleeding for their country's cause, and fighting against spiritual, intellectual and physical bondage.

But, sir, there is yet another thought that I wish to suggest now. We have had many sons and daughters who have come back here to-day, some who were never here before; but there has been some one here, too, who was also here a few years after the settlement of this place, and that is, the "Angel of Death." I could not go away, and do justice to my own feelings, if I did not call your attention to the fact that we have had a discourse—a sermon preached to us in the midst of our festivities. We have gathered here, this Autumnal day, and, in our joyousness, who thought the "angel reaper" so near, and ready to bear away another sheaf of his endless harvest? The falling leaf spoke to us of mortality, yet, perchance, we heeded not. We plaintively asked, in reference to your ancestors and the ministers who here once " dispensed the word " in this place—" Our fathers, where are they? and the prophets—do they live forever?" But, did our own mortality come here to us? Did we think death might be knocking at the very door of some of our tabernacles of clay, even when we were celebrating the memory of those who are gone? O, it could not be, that to-day we were to be greeted with that awful word of warning—to-day, in our joyousness, hear the solemn voice, saying : " Ye, too, must die!" And yet, so it is,—never are we exempt from the Destroyer's presence.

> " Leaves have their time to fall,
> And flowers to wither at the north wind's breath,
> And stars to set—but all,
> Thou hast all seasons for thine own, O Death! "

One who bore the name of one of the old settlers—the
14

name of Mirick—dropped dead to-day, and it seems as
though God had preached a lesson to us, and given to the
minister of this pulpit something to say next Sabbath—
something for me to say, and that I should be false to my
duty, if I did not say, that we are not only to remember
the fathers, but we are to remember that *we* are to meet
them soon. I have sought to do justice to the memory of
one, who, for a time, was falsely accused; see that you do
him justice, also. When I go up to the banks of the
Merrimac, in New Hampshire, and see the stone erected
there to the memory of the first minister of this place—a
man who deserves to be perpetually honored here, where
he so faithfully labored; who was not alone your minister,
but afterwards your representative in the Convention
which ratified our Federal Constitution, whose pro-slavery
clauses received his emphatic protest, and required his
reluctant vote against that instrument—I think the citizens
should remove that honored dust here, so that there may
be, not only the dust of one who had ministered here, but
especially of the one who first preached the Gospel in this
place; or, if it be too late for that, at least erect a fitting
memorial to him, in your church-yard, where the silent
dust of one of his children reposes. Were it needful, you
might call on me for my full proportion of pecuniary aid
in such a work as that. (Applause.)

My friends, you do indeed well to cherish the memory
of such fathers and mothers as I have sought to commemorate. For, changing the phraseology, if it could be done
so as to include heroic and holy women, as well as men,
what heart does not echo those familiar words : .

> " Lives of great men all remind us
> We can make our lives sublime,
> And, departing, leave behind us
> Footprints on the sands of time ;
>
> Footprints, that perhaps another-
> Sailing o'er life's solemn main,
> Some forlorn and shipwrecked brother,
> Seeing, shall take heart again.''

The Hon. CHARLES T. RUSSELL, of Boston, the Orator of the day, being called out, spoke as follows :

Mr. President :—I certainly concur most heartily in all that has been said—so well, so beautifully said—by my friend Fuller, who has just taken his seat, of the love for those who are gone, and, I may add, the love for those who are living. There is no place beyond my own fireside and home, that I visit with so much interest as this spot, where I received my birth, and where I received my early education; where I have always found sympathy and love, and honor, far beyond, I am afraid, what I deserve. And I desire here and now, and always, to thank the people of Princeton for the good they have done me by their institutions, and more than all, by their good and holy example. I had well hoped that, after my long, and, I fear, wearisome address this morning, I should not be called upon to speak to you again, at least to-day. When I was coming up here, a Princeton man told me a little anecdote, that may illustrate my position. He said, that some few years ago, he was called upon by a man to butcher a couple of hogs for him. They were enormous, raw-boned creatures, big enough to weigh five hundred pounds apiece, exactly what our old friend, now dead and gone, Mr. Zeke Davis, would call " working hogs." When he came to cut them, however, there was no pork thicker than that, (indicating by a measure of the finger,) in them. The butcher sent them home by a waggish boy of his, who, as he took them out of the wagon, said to the owner : " Mr. ———, don't you want to buy some good salt pork?" " No sir," said he, " what should I want to buy salt pork for ; have I not got these two hogs ? " " Well," said the boy, " I did not know *but you would like to get a little to fry yourn in.*" (Laughter.) I thought that by the time I got through that long address, with its propositions, like the dry bones in Ezekiel's vision, very many and very dry, you would want a little good pork to fry mine in, and would not call on me again. And I am happy to say, you have been eminently success-

ful, and that even the leanness and meagreness of my part
of the forenoon service, has been made very palatable, by
the rich and superb material in which you have this afternoon "fried it."

As I came up here, with an address prepared under the
pressure of so recent an invitation, I relied upon the same
security as that Princeton boy, who consoled his companion,
who, with torn pantaloons, was snivelling along home from
school. Said his sympathizing mate : "Have not you got
any good old grandmother at home, who will make all
straight there ?" So I knew, from long experience, I had
a most excellent and indulgent grandmother here, in my
native town, who would forgive anything herself, and
make anybody else forgive it, too.

I have, to-day, aimed only to tell you a plain and simple
story—homely, but not wholly useless and uninteresting to
us, I hope. I have felt, all day, much like apologizing to you
in the language of an old friend we all knew, now long dead
and gone, but whom you will recognize at once. He went
to one of the militia reviews, and when the inspector (I
believe I get the right officer—Major Cobb ?) came along,
presented his gun and accoutrements for examination.
Everything required by law and custom was there. There
was the priming-wire and brush, flint, box, and everything
to complete the equipment. "But," said the inspector,
"your gun looks rather rusty and black." "Yes," said he,
"I know it ; but I use it for hunting sometimes, and thought
it wa'nt best to *scour* it—make it *glammer* so it wouldn't kill
no squirrels." For the same reason, I came bringing the old
gun just as it was. I thought I wouldn't scour it, lest it
should "*glammer so*," I shouldn't even hit a squirrel with it.

Indeed, so rusty and old-fashioned am I, that I cannot
quite catch the step with all my young friends, who have
preceded me this evening, and who have spoken so
eloquently on their favorite topics. Much as I dislike the
evils of which some have spoken,—and I do, most exceed-
ingly,—I cannot quite agree with everything that has been

said upon men and measures. So you will allow me to dissent wherever I like, our's being a free atmosphere, and free highways, where every man is permitted to ride his own hobbyhorse, provided no one is asked to get up behind him. Perhaps I am like an old friend and townsman, in the memory of many younger than I am. For years he beat the martial drum here for the militia, so pleasantly alluded to by my friend, the poet, to-day. I I believe he did so, back, even, almost to Revolutionary days. All went well, till, in turn, the more enterprising youngsters got up the Light Infantry, in blue trousers and shiny buttons. They must needs have drumming of a more stirring, exciting, fashionable, quickstep style. So they got a modern drummer of skill, to their liking, who put in every modern beat, with all its fantastic elegance. You remember, Mr. President, how, one day, the old drummer stood in your store door, when the company went by, in all the gay movement of a recent march. "Ah!" said he, "Squire Russell, I like *the good old common time rub-a-dub-dub*; but Cobb puts in the flourishes—the Old Harry couldn't march after him." I cannot say how it may be with that distinguished personage. He is quite apt to get the lock step even with us, if we are not pretty careful when we put in our extra flourishes. Now, some of our young friends "put in the flourishes," of most modern style, and if I can't march after them, I hope it is not because I resemble the "Old Harry," but because old-fashioned and conservative, I prefer "*the good old common Revolutionary time rub-a-dub-dub.*"

Mr. President, some who have preceded me, have dwelt upon the ancient institutions of the town. Allow me a word, for what I may call some of the mediæval ones. My friend Wilder has spoken of his old school-master, Woods. I remember an old school-master here, too; and when I saw that same master, my friend Wilder himself, I seemed to sink right down into the little green petticoat I used to wear, and my perpendicular master stood right before me, teaching me my A B C. There was the very book, with all the pictures:

> " A, was an archer, and shot at a frog ;
> B, was a butcher, and kept a great dog."

Why, upon earth, the archer shot at such game, I could never understand ; it seemed to me poor business. If it would not have been a couplet that nobody would have believed, I always fancied it would have been:

> " A, was an archer, and shot at a peep,
> And B, was a butcher, and sold his meat cheap."

(Laughter.) Then came C; and he was

> " A captain all covered with lace."

That was our Captain Merriam.

> " D, was a drunkard, and had a red face."

That fellow was a stranger, and lived out of town, and only came up here "'Lection days ;" (laughter) and so on, to the end.

Then there was the now defunct Light Infantry. I remember the first time they came out. O, how my military admiration burst out at May training, and culminated in the sham fight, at Lancaster muster, when the Princeton boys put it to the Sterling fellows, to the last cartridge, and till they were all as dry of ammunition as the old continentals of Bunker Hill. We put it to them just as we have to the men of old Sutton, and Barre, and Marlboro', every Cattle-show day, for twenty-five years back, and just as we mean to for a hundred to come—only more. (Laughter and applause.)

Then there was the Engine Company. We had an engine once,—a distinguished citizen gave it to the town. I remember when it was brought out, and you, Mr. President, and Colonel Whitney, and Captain Dana and Merriam, and divers of those patriotic citizens around me, were at the brakes, and, I think, the late Mr. Boylston held the "nozzle." (Laughter.) So they worked at it, steady up and down, and it dreadfully screeched, and screamed, and squeaked, but not the drop of water would the ungrateful machine squirt. And so it went on, till a facetious townsman came along, and inquired whether that was " really an Ingun or only a Mulatto." (Laughter.)

Then there was the Singing School, kept by the father of our friend Howe, where I spent three days, trying to bring the singing of that excellent singer into harmony with mine. But I could never get, for one moment, his " fa, sol, la," to agree with my " fa, sol, la," howsoever I tried, so I gave it up; but not the Singing School. Ah, no! I could not forego that for mere musical disagreements. I went on to the end; and at the close of many a Winter evening, while they were pouring forth Coronation, Old Hundred, Dundee, or Plaintive Martyrs, (I couldn't exactly tell which,) in a harmony, compared with which, " Italian trills were tame," I was distressing myself with the embarrassing question, which young lady I should offer to go home with,—a question, sir, neither then nor now, among the rosy cheeks of these hills, so mighty easy of settlement, for a sensitive heart, just emerging from its teens. (Applause.) There was music here I could understand,—time, tune, scale and expression—" piano, dolce, affettuoso, lentando, pianissimo," from soft and plaintive, to the very softest.

Then, of an October evening, came the glorious huskings. That needs no description. What quantities of Indian pudding here, I stowed under my jacket, on some of these memorable occasions, at my good old grandfather's. In the remembrance of those boyish achievements, how annoyed I have sometimes been, at the capacity of the human organs, on extraordinary occasions.

Again, I have almost listened, since I came here, to hear the familiar old rattle of the six-horse Albany stage, going like lightning down yonder hill, with Joe Maynard on the box, cracking his whip over the leaders. And it was not till I recollected that it was Thursday, and not Wednesday, that I ceased to look about for old Basset's post, peddling some ten score of the " Massachusetts Spy," from West Boylston line to the boundaries of Westminster.

If I were to give you a sentiment, I would say :

The Institutions of Princeton—Not the ancient, nor the modern, but the *mediæval*,—the District School, the Light Infantry, the Engine Company, the Singing School, the Husking, and Joe Maynard and old Bassett's Stage.

And I think they were of a pretty good kind of institutions too. In the lighter frolics and humors of their day, our grandfathers and all about us participated. But they engaged in all these sports and amusements in a way consistent with a deep and fervent piety. They did not suppose that religion made men morose and unhappy, but induced a reverence for God and a respect for man. And thus, while we have ever had a moral and religious community, as such communities always are, I will venture to say there was not a happier, perhaps, I might say, merrier, community on the face of the earth. Certainly we boys can say that we did not suffer in that respect. But my time is quite gone, and I ought not to trespass another moment on your patience. I only add : Princeton —How I love her; God bless her forever. (Applause.)

Prof. EVERETT, the Poet of the day, was the next speaker. He said :

"I am no orator, as Brutus is;" but if ever I wished I were, it is at this moment. I have always been proud of being a son of Princeton, and to-day I have felt more proud than ever. When, three weeks ago, I received a request to prepare a poem for this occasion, I told my friends that, as Princeton had produced so many distinguished men, I felt greatly flattered by the compliment, and I felt the responsibility of a hundred years resting upon me.

Our venerable friend from Boston, (Mr. Wilder,) has referred to Master Woods, as an excellent teacher. I thank the gentleman, in behalf of the profession to which I have the honor to belong, for the merited compliments which he has paid to that profession. I left this town long since, and have been engaged in teaching, constantly providing laurels for the brows of others, though I have provided none for my own.

Last week I wrote to my brother, asking him to give me the names of all the ministers of the Gospel who have been born in this town. He gave me the names of nineteen. Last Saturday night, as I went to the Church Library, of which I happen to be the Librarian, a book was handed to me, called " *The Baptist Pulpit,*" by Dr. Sprague. In this work, he has given the names of the most distinguished ministers of that denomination who have lived in America. Among them I found the name of Rev. Dr. Abel Woods, the oldest son of Master Woods. Master·Woods had two sons who were Doctors of Divinity. Rev. Abel Woods, who began his ministry in 1790, and completed it in 1850, making a term of sixty years that he was in the Gospel ministry. His oldest son was President of a College, in Alabama, and now resides in Providence, Rhode Island. Dr. Leonard Woods was, for a long period, a Professor of Divinity, at Andover, and his son is a Doctor of Divinity, and President of a College. Then Master Woods had two sons who were Doctors of Divinity, and two grandsons who were also Doctors of Divinity. This is honor enough for one school-master.

I have one word to say about the mediæval institutions, to which reference has been made. We are here acting the part of Old Mortality. Those of you who are familiar with the writings of Walter Scott, will recollect how he represents Old Mortality, as going about in the grave-yards, raising up the fallen monuments, and etching out again the characters that had become indistinct, so that they might be easily read by the next generation. We, to-day, are going among

15

the graves of our fathers, etching out the letters, so that the next generation may read them, and hand them down for a hundred years more. God grant that their successors may do the same, and so on, till the last syllable of recorded time.

Let me refer to one institution, which has passed away, and which we would not revive. It was not peculiar to our fathers, but to the age. It was the institution of the Wine Cup. I recollect one personification of that institution, in old Mr. Elijah Rice. We all recollect him—the dear old man. Under that frock which he wore, although he sometimes carried a jug, he concealed as warm a heart as ever throbbed in a human bosom. Many a time have I sat in my father's barn, and heard him tell tales of the Revolution. The most noble ideas I have of Washington, were kindled at those huskings from the stories of old Elijah Rice. Had I half the powers of description which he possessed, I would relate one of them. Everybody, almost, used rum in those days; and one day when Mr. Rice was going home with his jug, he was met by Ephraim Beaman, Esq. He was always willing to be met anywhere. Mr. Beaman said, in a very hortatory manner, suitable to the occasion, "You love your worst enemy, Mr. Rice." "We are commanded to," was his quick response.

As I am the poet of the next hundred years, I will venture to read two brief odes, one of which, may represent the emotions with which our fathers regarded the wine cup, and the other, may represent our own feelings in regard to it.

THE BACCHANAL'S ODE.

Sweet soother of my cares and cure for all my pains,
 Whether thou mantlest with Hispania's treasure
Or juice from Rhine or brown Italian plains,
 Thou art a source of purest pleasure.
  When blithe Burns sang his Jeanie's praise
And brightened every feature,
  'Twas wine inspired his lays
And aided nature.

Hail sparkling Wine!
Far dearer than the Vine.
　I'll drink again
　My bright Champagne
　　Yet again!
　　Yet again!
It inspires my song,
Makes a short life long
　And a blessing,
　　A blessing,
　　A blessing.
　Still again
　I'll quaff amain
　With Bacchus' jolly train.
Till giddy, giddy, giddy,
　And quite unable
　　To hold my cup
　　Or e'en sit up,
The lamps all whirl round
And sleepy, sleepy, sleepy,
　I fall beneath the table
Or on the welcome ground
And sunk in soft repose, I sleep in peace profound.

THE BACCHANAL'S PALINODE.

Fell author of my cares and cause of all my pains,
　Whether thou temptest with Hispania's treasure
Or juice from Rhine or brown Italian plains,
　Thou poisonest every source of pleasure.
　Where Burns sung Highland Mary's praise,
And colored every feature,
　Wine ne'er inspired his lays
Or aided Nature.
　　No: dearer are the Nine
　　Than the most sparkling Wine.
　　　I'll ne'er drink again
　　　That cursed Champagne!
　·　　　Ne'er again,
　　　　Ne'er again,
　　　It hampers my verse,
　　　It makes life a curse.
　　　　And a burden,
　　　　A burden,
　　　　A burden.

I never again
Will fever my brain,
With Bacchus' swinish train,
Till giddy, giddy, giddy,
And quite unable
To hold my cup
Or e'en sit up
The lamps all whirl round,
And sleepy, sleepy, sleepy,
I fell beneath the table
Or on the cold hard ground,
And lie in dead oblivion lost and sleep profound.

Mr. EVERETT, (Toast-Master):—With your permission, I will now make a motion, full of solemn interest to all. We have reviewed to-day, the century that has just passed, and have looked into the graves of our fathers and mothers, and our grandfathers and grandmothers. I move that, after we have listened to the closing hymn, we adjourn to the call of posterity, one hundred years hence.

The motion was unanimously carried, and the following hymn, composed by William E. Richardson, of Boston, a native of Princeton, was sung, as the closing exercise. Tune—"Auld Lang Syne."

HYMN.

BY WILLIAM E. RICHARDSON.

Here gathered round this festive scene,
Have met the friends of youth,
To pledge once more affection's gift
Of Friendship, Love and Truth ;
  Then ere our festive scenes are o'er,
  Ere we our joys resign,
  With hand in hand, each trusty friend
  Shall pledge to " auld lang syne."

We'll pledge their memories, who of old,
Could home and joys forego,
Who dared to found for us a home,
One hundred years ago ;

Here on this spot their children met,
To join with loud acclaim,
With grateful hearts to twine a wreath
Around their honored name.

Old age here blends its trembling tongue,
With childhood's lisping vow,
To join the song whose echoes ring,
Round old Wachusett's brow ;
    Then swell the chorus to their praise,
    Join every one below,
    In memory of our parents dead,
    One hundred years ago.

Time will not grant a scene like this,
To us on earth again,
Then while we pledge the parting tear,
We'll trust in " auld lang syne ; "
    Then may our record brightly shine,
    Prove earthly duties done,
    'Twill gild the page of past " lang syne,"
    And gem the one to come.

LETTERS.

The following letters were received by the Committee of Arrangements, from individuals invited, but unable to be present on the occasion of the Anniversary.

WESTBOROUGH, Oct. 15th, 1859.

W. B. GOODNOW :

Dear Sir:—It would afford me great pleasure to be present at the commemorative Centennial Anniversary of Princeton. Did not indispensable engagements prevent my attendance, I would most cordially accept your invitation. In token of the deep interest I still cherish for the people of your town, I offer the following sentiment :

Princeton—Elevated and commanding in its natural position. May its inhabitants, in time to come, as in time past, be distinguished for their physical and intellectual vigor; for firmness of purpose, and for the industrious cultivation of its mountain soil.

Yours, truly,

E. DEMOND.

UXBRIDGE, Oct. 15th, 1859.

WILLIAM B. GOODNOW, Esq. :

My Dear Sir:—Your circular, inviting me to attend the Centennial Celebration in Princeton, on the 20th inst., was duly received. I am very grateful for this kind remembrance of the Committee of Arrangements, signified by yourself. It would give me great pleasure to be present on an occasion of so much interest to the citizens of Princeton. I was longer in the ministry there than were any of my predecessors, or than have been any of my successors. It was the birth-place of my children. Though I have been away many years, my interest in, and attachment to the place and inhabitants, have not ceased. But I am now very much of an invalid. I have not strength to enable me to endure the excitement and fatigue of the occasion, which I very much regret. I shall always rejoice in the temporal and spiritual prosperity of the inhabitants of Princeton, where I spent so many years, and had so many firm friends,—friends, many of whom have passed to the better land.

With kind regards to your associates on the Committee, and hoping the occasion will pass pleasantly and profitably, I remain, dear sir,

Respectfully, yours,

SAMUEL CLARKE.

ELLINGTON, Oct. 18th, 1859.

To MESSRS. EDWARD E. HARTWELL, JOHN BROOKS, JR., GEORGE E. PRATT, and others, Committee of Princeton, Mass., appointed to direct and superintend the public proceedings in that town, on the 20th inst., in commemoration of the completion of *one hundred years* since the incorporation of the town.

GENTLEMEN :

Yours of the 15th inst., through the agency of Caleb Dana, Esq., of Worcester, came to hand *last eve*, (the one directed to me in Troy, I never heard from,) is a call upon me for my thanks for your kind and polite attention to me, in desiring my attendance on the interesting occasion,—an invitation I should most readily accept, if I had strength and health equal to the journey and the fatigues which must attend it. But, as my health *is*, I cannot think of it. On the first of May, 1859, I entered on my eighty-fifth year, and all will say, as relates to a man thus *advanced*, that *home is* the proper place for him.

With my best respects for you, gentlemen, personally, and my cordial desire that the occasion may bring together many circles of relatives, located abroad, and large numbers not related, now almost strangers, from long absence from the family mansion ; and that the festivities and exercises of the day, may be blessed for the highest good of the town, and every family in it, is the warm desire and earnest prayer of, gentlemen, yours, most respectfully,

JOSEPH RUSSELL.

www.ingramcontent.com/pod-product-compliance
Lightning Source LLC
Chambersburg PA
CBHW030627270326
41927CB00007B/1341